The Illustrated Lives of the Great Composers.

Stravinsky

Neil Wenborn

OMNIBUS PRESS

London/New York/Sydney

For Sue and Henry

Cover design and art direction by Pearce Marchbank, Studio Twenty
Text design by Hilite
Picture research by Nikki Lloyd & Lisa Quas

ISBN: 0.7119.7651.1
Order No: OP 48134

Exclusive Distributors
Book Sales Limited,
8/9 Frith Street,
London W1V 5TZ, UK.

Music Sales Corporation,
257 Park Avenue South,
New York, NY 10010, USA.

Five Mile Press,
22 Summit Road,
Noble Park,
Victoria 3174,
Australia.

To the Music Trade only:
Music Sales Limited,
8/9, Frith Street,
London W1V 5TZ, UK.

Photo credits:

Milein Cosman/Lebrecht: 162,172,173; Mary Evans Picture Library: 20,29,39,41,48,
50t,53,56,146; Fotomas Index: 18,44t; Hulton Getty: 110,120,138,148,160,169,174,
176,178,184,191; Lebrecht Collection: 3,11,13,14,17,24,30,34,44b,45,47,49,58,59t&b,
65,66,69t&b,70,71,73,75,76,78,82,84,86,87,90,95,98,100,103,104, 105,106,109,117,118,
123,126,134,142,151,153,155,164,185,193,194; Novosti: 15,21,33,55,80,182; Sotheby's:
19,50b,51t&b,60,64,74; Horst Tappe/Lebrecht: 186.
page 60 -The Rite of Spring - Stravinsky © Copyright 1912, 1921 by Hawkes & Son
(London) Ltd; page 106 - Oedipus Rex - Stravinsky © Copyright 1927 by Hawkes & Son
(London) Ltd. Revised version: © Copyright 1949, 1950 by Hawkes & Son (London) Ltd.
U.S. Copyright Renewed; Both reprinted by permission of Boosey & Hawkes Music
Publishers. Page 84 - Cover of Stravinsky's 'Ragtime' © Succession Picasso/DACS 1999.
Page 76 - Sketch of Stravinsky ©Succession Picasso/DACS 1999. Page 98 - Stravinsky
rehearsing Sacre Du Printemps by Jean Cocteau © ADAGP, Paris and DACS, London 1999.
Page 86 - Stravinsky and Picasso by Jean Cocteau © ADAGP, Paris and DACS, London 1999.

Printed and bound in Great Britain by Redwood Books Ltd, Trowbridge.

A catalogue record for this book is available from the British Library.

Visit Omnibus Press at www.omnibuspress.co.uk

Contents

Preface

Igor Stravinsky was probably the most influential figure in the musical life of the twentieth century. He was certainly one of the most controversial. Catapulted to international fame by his ballet *The Firebird* at the age of 28, he went on to produce a corpus of around 100 works which radically altered the direction of contemporary music and divided opinion throughout the musical world.

These works are generally grouped into three periods – the 'Russian', the 'neo-classical' and the 'serial' – but while such divisions may follow the broad contours of Stravinsky's musical development, they also serve to mask the essentially protean nature of his talent. Never fully satisfied with what he had achieved, and more interested in the act of creation than in the catalogue of his works, Stravinsky can be said to have reinvented himself with each new composition. Certainly, there can be few composers in the history of music, and none of equivalent stature, whose output is so stylistically various while at the same time so wholly and consistently characteristic. Like his friend and colleague Pablo Picasso, with whom he has often been compared, Stravinsky can seem to be many different artists, but is always finally and unmistakably himself. His creative career lasted more than 60 years. But from the riots which greeted the first performance of *The Rite of Spring* in Paris in 1913 to the chorus of bewilderment and anger with which his last great serial works were received in many quarters in the 1950s and 1960s, he continued to confound and astonish by his capacity for self-renewal, remaining constantly one step ahead of critics and supporters alike.

At the heart of Stravinsky's music, as in the character of the man himself, lies a deep dichotomy between energy and constraint. A meticulously disciplined composer – he once said he identified with Van Eyck, who would labour for months with a magnifying glass to paint a perfect beetle – he could produce music of such visceral force as *The Rite of Spring* or the *Symphony in Three Movements*; and while famously denying that music could express anything at all, he created some of the most deeply felt devotional works of the twentieth century, as well as such lyrical masterpieces as *Apollo* and the neglected 'melodrama' *Persephone*.

Similarly, he was in life at once a highly driven and a highly guarded personality. Few composers have lived so long in the spotlight of publicity. But for all the films and recordings, for all the hundreds of thousands of words written by and about him since he first burst onto the international stage in 1910, Stravinsky the man remains a strangely elusive figure. Not only do his own writings on life and music conceal as often as they illuminate; many of the most important are mediated through the voices of others. The *Poetics of Music*, his most extended treatise on his own art, was drafted by the composer Roland-Manuel, and many of his published statements on individual works were actually written by friends and associates. The primary published sources on his life are also partly the work of others: the *Autobiography* was largely ghosted by his friend Walter Nouvel, once the company secretary of Diaghilev's Ballets Russes; and the invaluable series of 'conversation books' which appeared from the late 1950s were jointly produced with the great Stravinsky scholar Robert Craft, who was effectively a member of Stravinsky's family circle for the last 23 years of the composer's life. Craft, to whom any biographer of Stravinsky must owe an incalculable debt, has also published, under the title *Stravinsky: Chronicle of a Friendship*, the diary he kept during the years of his closest association with the composer – a document the immediacy and elegance of which justifies the title of Stravinsky's Boswell so often, if somewhat misleadingly, accorded him. A longer list of Craft's publications with and about Stravinsky, which also include a three-volume selection from the composer's voluminous correspondence, is given in *Further Reading* on page 195.

Given the centrality of the conversation books and the *Autobiography* as first-hand sources – and in the case of Stravinsky's earlier Russian years almost the only sources – most published accounts of the composer's life have drawn heavily on them, either in summary or by direct quotation. This book is no exception, and the author and publishers would like to thank the originators of all those sources for permission to include the quotations made in the text.

As far as possible, throughout the book Russian names have been transliterated according to a consistent convention. However, for the greater part of his life Stravinsky was an exile from the Russia of his birth, first in Europe and later in Hollywood, and many of the key figures in his biography were either also exiles or cosmopolites who adopted the forms and conventions most appropriate to the circles in which they lived and worked; indeed, Stravinsky himself used different forms of his name at different stages of his career. We have therefore preferred familiarity to consistency where it would seem artificial to do otherwise: for example, Serge Diaghilev is preserved in place of the purer Sergey Dyagilev, and Alexandre Benois in place of Aleksandr Benua. For the most part, the style of Russian names thus follows that used in the *Oxford Dictionary of Music*.

The titles of Stravinsky's works are given in English, with the French version, where it is also current, in brackets after the first major reference (for example *The Rite of Spring* (*Le Sacre du printemps*)). In those very few cases where the English version is seldom used (for example, *Jeu de cartes*), the English is given in brackets after the first major reference. No attempt has been made to include transliterations of Russian titles, except where the French and English versions of a title are both virtually unused (for example, *Zvezdoliki*).

The style of quotations is of course left unchanged, even where it conflicts with the conventions just outlined.

Another complication confronting any biographer of Stravinsky is the difference between the Old Style (Julian) and New Style (Gregorian) calendars. The nature of the complication is explained in the first chapter (see page 11); it is worth noting here, though, that the New Style calendar has been used throughout, except where the text indicates otherwise or where it is unclear which calendar is intended.

Like the other titles in this series, this book makes no attempt at detailed musicological analysis. Rather, it seeks to set Stravinsky's music in the context of his life, and his life in the context of his times. Those times were a vortex of artistic, social and geopolitical change, in which Stravinsky was deeply involved, both as subject and as shaper. Relentlessly gregarious when not in the throes of composition, he counted among his friends a glittering cross-section of the century's social and cultural elite, from Diaghilev and Cocteau to Auden and Picasso, from Chaplin and Hitchcock to the old aristocracy of Europe, and his biography touches milieux as various as the drawing rooms of Tsarist St Petersburg, the studios of the great Hollywood movie magnates, and the reception suites of the White House and the Kremlin. This book traces the course of a remarkable creative career which spanned the convulsive final years of Imperial Russia and the social ferment of 1960s America, and served to establish Stravinsky not only as the most celebrated composer of his time but also as one of the defining forces of twentieth-century culture.

Chapter 1

Early life (1882-1902)

'I do not like to remember my childhood,' Stravinsky told his long-time friend and associate Robert Craft, abruptly deflecting discussion of his early life. Elsewhere, he likened childhood to extreme old age as 'a time of humiliations' and described it, with unconcealed bitterness, as 'a period of waiting for the moment when I could send everyone and everything connected with it to hell.'

More than a century after Stravinsky's birth, it is impossible to uncover the springs of this implacable resentment. It is hard enough just to piece together the fractured chronology of his formative years. Most of what we know about Stravinsky's first two decades derives from his *Autobiography* and from scattered reminiscences in the 'conversation books' published in the last years of his life. But both are at least partly the work of others, and both, by their very nature, are highly subjective accounts, committed to paper long after the events concerned; even the order of those events is not always clear or consistent, either internally or with what little external evidence has come down to us. What's more, Stravinsky was, in life as in music, a great wearer of masks, and the image presented by his recollections, and especially his earliest recollections, is a conspicuously crafted one. Nowhere, then, is his much-remarked elusiveness more apparent than in respect of his childhood and adolescence. In this most documented of lives, the events of the early years remain obstinately dateless, visible only through a haze of impressions, evasions, supposition.

Igor Fyodorovich Stravinsky was born at midday on 17 June 1882 in the Russian seaside village of Oranienbaum on the Gulf of Finland. Even this apparently straightforward information, however, immediately needs to be qualified.

First of all, there is the difference between the Old Style (Julian) and New Style (Gregorian) calendars. The date of birth according to the Old Style calendar, which was in use in

Igor Stravinsky aged 18 months

Russia until 1918, was 5 June; and to complicate matters still further, the difference between the two calendars increased by one day per century. Stravinsky therefore celebrated his birthday on 18 June for the greater part of his life. Secondly, Oranienbaum was renamed Lomonosov during the Soviet era – a reminder, if one were needed, of how radical a divide the 1917 Revolution was to prove for Russians of Stravinsky's generation, and how critical in determining the course of his own future career. And finally, Oranienbaum was not even his home town; after that summer, he saw it again only during his momentous visit to the USSR at the age of 80. His parents were simply renting a house there for their summer holiday. Together with Igor's two older brothers Roman (eight) and Yury (three), they lived some 40 kilometres to the west in St Petersburg (subsequently Petrograd and Leningrad and now St Petersburg again), where the new baby was formally baptised into the Russian Orthodox church on 11 July.

The Stravinsky family were well-to-do, cultured and conservative. Descended from Polish landowners, Igor's father, Fyodor Stravinsky, was the principal bass at the Mariinsky Theatre, the imperial opera house in St Petersburg and hub of cultural life in the Russian capital. He was famous for his dramatic roles, and was much admired as a singer and actor by the leading musicians of his day, including Tchaikovsky, at whose funeral he was to be a pall-bearer. Fyodor had discovered his musical vocation while reading law at university in Odessa and Kiev, and subsequently studied music at the St Petersburg Conservatoire, making his debut at the Mariinsky six years before Igor's birth, as Mephistopheles in Gounod's *Faust*. A man of broad literary interests, he was well-connected throughout St Petersburg's artistic community, and his huge private library, which included numerous musical scores, was important enough to be declared a national collection by Lenin's Bolshevik government. He was a personal friend of Turgenev and Dostoyevsky, and Mussorgsky and Rimsky-Korsakov were among the regular visitors to the Stravinskys' third-floor flat at 66 Krukov (subsequently Griboyedova) Canal.

According to Stravinsky, however, Fyodor was also an aloof and disciplinarian figure, given to disturbing outbreaks of rage, and Igor's early years were shadowed by fear of him. Painfully illuminating is his account, in *Dialogues*, of how 'as a child alone in my room, I once saw my father instead of myself in the looking-glass, and my already strong case of father-fears became mirror-fears as well'. Seventy-five years later, the very word 'mirror' still frightened him. That said, it is inevitably

Fyodor Stravinsky (1843-1902),
the subject of Igor's 'father fears'

Stravinsky's side of the story which has come down to us.
Fyodor's diary, by contrast, shows a man generally happy in his
work and marriage and wishing the same blessings on his
children. Robert Craft has noted the striking similarity
between the two men's handwriting, and Stravinsky himself
compared his own touchiness before public performances with
that of his father. Nor did the parallels end there. Stravinsky
inherited Fyodor's violent temper and would prove just as
tyrannical a father to his own children. Perhaps the true cause
of friction lay in too great a similarity of temperament.

The composer's mother, Anna Kirillovna (*née* Kholodovsky),
was the daughter of a minister of agriculture in Kiev, where she
met Fyodor during his stint at the city's opera house. The young
Igor found her no more approachable than his father; indeed,
he thought it her mission in life to torment him. She seems
never to have appreciated his music, and even when he was 40
years old and one of the world's most celebrated living
composers, would publicly take him to task for 'criticising your
betters' (by which she meant St Petersburg's 'local genius',

Scriabin). Stravinsky claimed never to have felt more than a sense of duty towards her. Even in adulthood, however, he remained fearful enough of her bad opinion to conceal those aspects of his private life of which he knew she would disapprove – notably his long affair with Vera de Bosset, who was to become his second wife.

Nor did the young Stravinsky – 'Ghima' to his family – feel any closer to his older siblings. He admired his eldest brother Roman, whom photographs show as a dashing young man in cadet uniform, but the gap in years and interests was too great to be bridged before Roman's early death in 1897. Despite the relative closeness in age, his brother Yury too was a marginal figure in Stravinsky's childhood and as adults the brothers never met after 1912. Yury remained in Soviet Russia after the Revolution, and pursued a successful career as a structural engineer, dying in Leningrad shortly before the German blockade of 1941.

Stravinsky aged three and a half

Among the members of his immediate family, it was only in Gury, the Stravinskys' fourth son, born in 1884, that the young Igor found a companion capable of giving him the love and understanding he felt their parents denied them, though even here he felt unable wholly to shed what his wife Vera would later memorably describe as 'the carapace over the feelings'. Gury was the only other Stravinsky son to have inherited Fyodor's musical talent. He took singing lessons and from 1912 to 1914 was a professional baritone in a private theatre in St Petersburg. Stravinsky wrote two settings of poems by Verlaine for him in 1910, and was grief-stricken by news of his death from typhus while serving on the Southern Front in 1917.

As in many an upper-middle-class household of the time, the affection of the servants went some way towards compensating for the parents' perceived remoteness. Years later, Stravinsky would recall the protective friendship of the family retainer, Simon Ivanovich, who shared a cubby-hole under the stairs with stacks of Fyodor's books, and the sense of security he felt with their Finnish cook, Caroline. He was closest of all to his nurse Bertha, whose voice, he said, was the most loving he ever heard in his childhood and whom he later recruited as nanny to his own children. (She was still in the composer's service in Switzerland at the time of her death in 1917, which he openly admitted affected him far more deeply than that of his own mother some years later.) It is particularly significant that Bertha spoke German with her young ward. From his earliest years, Stravinsky's essential Russianness was informed by a wider European culture.

14

The pattern of the family's life was as regular as the seasons it followed. The year was typically divided between St Petersburg and the large rural estates of Stravinsky's numerous aunts and uncles. The summer was spent in the country, the winter in town.

Summers were a time of cousins, picnics, sketching and amateur dramatics. They were also the time to which Stravinsky ascribed his earliest musical memories. One of the first of these, if his recollections are to be trusted, was of a large, red-haired, bearded old peasant sitting on a stump of a tree, wearing birch sandals and a red shirt. He was dumb, Stravinsky tells us, and the children were afraid of him. Nonetheless, curiosity would draw them to him, and then:

'to amuse them, he would begin to sing. This song was composed of two syllables, the only ones he could pronounce. They were devoid of any meaning, but he made them alternate with incredible dexterity in a very rapid tempo. He used to accompany this clucking in the following way: pressing the palm of his right hand under his left armpit, he would work his left arm with a rapid movement, making it press on the right hand. From beneath the red shirt he extracted a succession of sounds which were somewhat dubious but very rhythmic, and which might be euphemistically described as resounding kisses.'

The young Igor would imitate this music at home, but when forbidden the 'indecent' actions claims to have lost all interest

15

in the unaccompanied syllables. As with other such recollections, however, there is an artfulness in the description which invites scepticism. The fascination with rhythm, the interest in syllables independent of meaning, the delight in the unconventional, the insistence on the indivisibility of the musical idea – they all connect a little too neatly with the outlook of the mature Stravinsky.

Another early memory is of a crowd of women singing in unison as they returned from work in a neighbouring village. Stravinsky claimed to have been so struck by the tune that he remembered it perfectly, singing it to his parents when he got home and receiving in the process a rare compliment on the trueness of his ear. If, as Stravinsky suggests, this recollection dates from before his third birthday, it is a remarkable harbinger of future talent. But again there are grounds for suspicion. There is, after all, little external evidence of musical precocity in the young Stravinsky to corroborate such reminiscences. Indeed, his first two decades of life must surely count as among the slightest in musical achievement of any major composer, and his parents – who, whatever their shortcomings, might reasonably have been expected to recognise musicianship when they saw it – actively encouraged him to pursue a different career. For all his claims that he was aware of it from earliest childhood, the roots of his vocation remain elusive.

However selective his musical memories of them, there can be no doubt that two of the places visited by the Stravinskys during these summers were to have a special significance in Igor's life. The first was Pavlovka, a vast estate of farms and forests in the Samara Government, which was owned by his uncle Alexander Yelachich and which the boy first visited in 1885. Much as he disliked the bullying of his Yelachich cousins, he found his uncle's devotion to music highly congenial and became an enthusiastic participant in the family's piano duets. He also claimed that Yelachich was the only member of his family to recognise his musical talent. A civil service general and a somewhat eccentric figure, Yelachich idolised Brahms and Beethoven, and would sometimes spend days at a time playing the piano. Stravinsky waxed poetic over the pleasures of the river journey to Pavlovka, which took four days along the Volga, describing them as among the happiest days of his life. However, since he also says that his second visit took place only when he was 21, most of his memories of music-making with his favourite uncle must be of the latter's town house in St Petersburg.

Waiting to send them all to hell:
Stravinsky in 1897, aged 15

The second summer destination which was to have an important influence on the composer's future life was Pechisky in the western Ukraine. It was on this estate, owned by Dr Gabriel Nossyenko – like Yelachich the husband of one of Igor's mother's sisters – that he discovered, during the summers of 1891 and 1892, the rapport with his cousin Catherine Nossyenko which would lead, 15 years later, to their marriage. (His connection with the Nossyenkos also led to his first acquaintance with Ustilug, a village in Volhynia on the Polish border where his uncle acquired an estate at around the same time and where Igor spent most of the summers of his adolescence with his brother Gury. Ustilug was to become the composer's own summer home from shortly after his marriage until the outbreak of the First World War.) Another memory of his Pechisky summers was visiting the great fair at nearby Yarmolintsi, where he revelled in the bright costumes of the peasants and the dancing competitions which introduced him to some of the traditional dances he was later to incorporate into *Petrushka*.

It was at Pechisky too that Stravinsky's brother Roman died suddenly in 1897, apparently from the after-effects of a childhood attack of diphtheria. His parents were devastated, and Fyodor never fully recovered from the tragedy. Roman's death struck Igor deeply too, not just as the loss of a brother of whom, despite their lack of common interests, he was proud, but also as further fuel for that sense of alienation to which he was to ascribe at least part of his urge to excel at music. 'My unhappiness' he later wrote,

'so I have always been accustomed to think, was the result of my father's remoteness and my mother's denial of affection. Then when my eldest brother died suddenly, and my mother did not transfer any of her feelings for him to me, and my father did not become any less aloof, I resolved (a resolution made at some time and for one reason or another by all children) that someday I would show them.'

If an overwhelming commitment to music hardly emerges from the pattern of Stravinsky's life at this time, other traits of the future composer certainly do. His lifelong hypochondria was already apparent, fostered by his parents' conviction that he was a sickly child – he claims to have spent much of his time sequestered in the 'Petrushka's cell' of a room he shared with Gury – and by the fact that his father showed him affection only when he was ill. According to his second wife, Vera, he developed his taste for medicines at the age of five, when he

The Nevsky Prospect,
St Petersburg

would climb up to his parents' medical cabinet to experiment with their array of medicinal herbs. In later life he took his temperature at least once a day, was always trying out the latest health or dietary fad, and would install shelfloads of remedies in his hotel rooms as a shield against actual and potential ailments.

Stravinsky's closeness with money is also evident from early letters, in which, long before his income actually felt the pinch of war and revolution, he would detail every kopek of his daily expenditure. This habit too continued into later life. One of the least sympathetic strands in his correspondence is the tight financial rein on which he kept his mother and his first wife, even when the latter was suffering in a French sanatorium from the tuberculosis which would eventually kill her. Paradoxically, this miserliness coexisted with extravagant personal tastes, not least in clothes and wine, and with a generosity towards friends and extended family which would lead to his supporting numerous dependants.

In some of the smallest things, too, the patterns set during these years persisted into later life. Particularly poignant is the fact that, even in extreme old age, Stravinsky always insisted on having a night-light in his room – a reflection, at almost a century's distance, of the street light outside the Krukov Canal apartment which kept at bay the night-fears of his earliest childhood.

18

Stravinsky's family life there may have been troubled, but St Petersburg itself remained dearer to him than any other city in the world – 'so much a part of my life' he wrote in his seventies, 'that I am almost afraid to look further into myself, lest I discover how much of me is still joined to it'. Stravinsky's descriptions of the sights, the smells and above all the sounds of the imperial capital are among the most evocative passages in all the conversation books. He recalls with lyrical zest the grating of the iron wheels of droshkies on cobblestones or parquetry pavements, the cracking whips of the coachmen, the cries of the street-vendors and knife-grinders, the 'cannonade of bells' from the Nikolsky Cathedral, the trilling of a café balalaika band, even the 'musique concrète' of the first St Petersburg telephones – the Stravinskys' apartment was one of the first to be connected – which sounded, he said, like the opening of the second act of his opera *The Nightingale*.

Vivid to his memory too were the smells of tar, leather and horses, of the felt hood he was forced to wear during the winter months, of Mahorka tobacco, of the gas and kerosene lamps of his largely indoor childhood. He recalled with love the Italianate ochres of the city's public buildings, the blue and gold interior of the Mariinsky, the bustle and life of the broad Nevsky Prospect, the glare of the snow in winter and the light of the aurora borealis in spring, bright enough at times for him to work by it into the early hours of the morning.

This was a city of canals, islands and rivers, over which the young Igor would watch the sleighs whisking in winter or the

'The violent Russian spring that seemed to begin in an hour and was like the whole earth cracking': *Ice Breaking on the Neva* by Anna Petrovna Lebedeva

19

gulls dipping as fish surfaced with the rising water levels of the spring. He loved to skate on the frozen Neva, or be towed across on a sleigh by the Finnish peasants who descended on St Petersburg during the winter months. It was, as he remembered it in exile, 'a realistic fairy-tale world whose lost beauty I have tried to rediscover later in life', not least through the stories of Hans Christian Andersen, the basis for his opera *The Nightingale* and his ballet *The Fairy's Kiss*.

It was also, of course, the nerve centre of the great Russian empire, and the Tsar was often to be seen there. Igor remembered one brilliant procession, a parade honouring the Shah of Persia, at which the 'long, forest-like noise, the "hurrah" of the crowds in the streets, [came] in crescendo waves closer and closer with the approaching isolated car of the Tsar and the Shah'. On other occasions, he glimpsed Alexander III occupying 'the whole front seat of a droshky driven by a troika coachman as big and obese as himself. The coachman… was seated in front of the Tsar, but elevated on the driver's seat where his enormous behind, like a gigantic pumpkin, was only a few inches from the Tsar's face.' The 13-year-old Stravinsky also attended Alexander's lying-in-state in the cathedral of SS Peter and Paul, and the sight of the yellowed body in the open coffin haunted him for the rest of his life.

Perhaps above all, St Petersburg was a city annually transformed by the passage of the seasons. With the advent of spring, the frozen waterways would fracture explosively as the ice-bound capital thawed into the 'Venice of the north'. When Robert Craft asked the septuagenarian composer what he most loved about the Russia of his earliest years, his reply was unequivocal: 'The violent Russian spring that seemed to begin in an hour and was like the whole earth cracking. That was the most wonderful event of every year of my childhood.' The connection with *The Rite of Spring* – perhaps his most famous single work – was surely no more lost on the composer than it has been on his biographers.

Whatever the position of music among the young Stravinsky's summer entertainments, here in St Petersburg it was central to the family's life. From his room, Igor could hear his father practising his operatic roles and from the windows of the flat could see stage scenery being transported along the Krukov Canal by barge to the Mariinsky Theatre. He was a frequent visitor to the Mariinsky, and once told an interviewer: 'I spent my childhood on the stage of the opera, where my love of music was born.' It was here that he saw his first opera, Glinka's *A Life for the Tsar*, though he dates the occasion

Pytor Tchaikovsky (1840-1893), who remained one of Stravinsky's musical heroes

variously to the age of seven or eight and to a (surely later) time when he already knew the work from the piano score. Whenever it was, he was overcome with joy at the sound of the orchestra, the first he had ever heard. The music made an indelible impression on him and he remained a lifelong devotee of Glinka, from whom, he would later say, 'all music in Russia stems'.

It was at the Mariinsky too that the young Stravinsky saw his first ballet, Tchaikovsky's *The Sleeping Beauty*. He also attended, in 1893, the fiftieth anniversary gala performance of Glinka's *Russlan and Lyudmila*, in which his father was playing Farlaf. During the interval, his mother pointed out, in the foyer behind their box, 'a man with white hair, large shoulders, a corpulent back'. It was Tchaikovsky. For the rest of his life, Stravinsky was to treasure this passing glimpse of the composer who was to remain one of his musical heroes. Just two weeks later, Tchaikovsky was dead and the Mariinsky swathed in black for a memorial concert at which the composer's last symphony, the *Pathétique*, was performed in tribute. The 11-year-old Stravinsky was once more in the audience, and it was to this time that he later dated 'the beginning of [his] conscious life as artist and musician'. By the age of 16, with the benefit of a pass from

'I spent my childhood on the stage of the opera': the Mariinsky Theatre, St Petersburg, where Igor's father Fyodor was principal bass'

his father, he was spending five or six nights a week at the Mariinsky, attending rehearsals and performances and cultivating friendships among the principal singers and intrumentalists, one of whom fostered his lifelong addiction to nicotine by procuring cigarettes for him.

Stravinsky's formal musical education, however, began only at the age of nine when his parents arranged piano lessons for him. His first teacher was a Mlle A P Snetkova, the daughter of a violinist in the Mariinsky Theatre orchestra; his second Mlle L A Kashperova, who had been a pupil of the great Russian virtuoso and founder of the St Petersburg Conservatoire, Anton Rubinstein. In his published recollections, Stravinsky was waspish about both women. He claimed to have learnt nothing at all from Mlle Snetkova. As for Mlle Kashperova, she was 'an excellent pianist and a blockhead', whose 'narrowness and… formulae greatly encouraged the supply of bitterness that accumulated in my soul until, in my mid-twenties, I broke loose and revolted from her and from every stultification in my studies, my schools, and my family'. In his time with the latter, however, he made sufficient progress to be able to play Mendelssohn's G minor *Piano Concerto,* as well as numerous classical sonatas. Her tuition also enabled him to pursue his study of operas in piano score, including those of Wagner, whose work he loved at this stage of his life as much as he would later deplore it. Furthermore, they awoke in him a passion for improvisation from which was to derive his lifelong habit of composing at the piano. Perhaps it is not too fanciful either to see in the textural clarity of Stravinsky's scores a legacy of Mlle Kashperova's eccentric embargo on the sustaining pedal. Whatever her influence, though, Stravinsky was never to become an outstanding pianist, a fact which no doubt weighed with his parents in directing his higher education.

It is unclear from his own reminiscences when he began to take lessons in theory and composition, but it may have been around this time that he enrolled with his first harmony teacher, the composer Fyodor Akimenko, whom it is no surprise to learn Stravinsky found 'unsympathetic'. His next teacher was Vassily Kalafaty, another composer, whom he described as 'a small, black-faced Greek with huge black moustaches' and with whom he studied counterpoint and harmony for two years. Conservative in his musical tastes and terse almost to silence, he was a demanding tutor and clearly left his mark on the future composer. 'Kalafaty taught me to appeal to my ear as the first and last test, and for that I am grateful', Stravinsky was to write in *Expositions and*

Developments. Compared with Stravinsky's judgements of his other early mentors, it is a rare accolade.

Another influence on his musical development at this stage was one Ivan Pokrovsky, a man some eight years older than Stravinsky, whom he met while he was still at school and who steered him towards an appreciation of French music and culture. Under Pokrovsky's quasi-bohemian tutelage, Stravinsky got to know the works of Gounod, Bizet, Delibes and Chabrier, playing through their operas in four-hand piano reductions. From 1897 to 1899 the two were inseparable friends.

Stravinsky was now beginning to compose small pieces for piano – the headmaster of his secondary school was to reprimand him for it – and was clearly seeking guidance from outside the family on his chances of pursuing a musical career. An early idol was Glazunov, the toast of the Russian musical establishment since his precocious symphonic debut 15 years earlier, and in 1897 Stravinsky transcribed one of the older composer's string quartets for piano and took it to his house to show him. Despite knowing Stravinky's father, Glazunov received him ungraciously, thumbed through his manuscript and cursorily told him it was unmusical. The 15-year-old went away thoroughly discouraged. As Aldous Huxley was later to observe, Stravinsky had an 'elephant's memory' for even imaginary slights, and no doubt his later vituperative dismissal of Glazunov owes something to this adolescent rejection.

Another of his boyhood heroes was Nikolay Rimsky-Korsakov, a friend of his father's and one of Russia's most venerated composers. It is uncertain when the two first met, but he was already a familiar figure to Stravinsky by the time he was formally introduced at a rehearsal of Rimsky's opera *Sadko* in St Petersburg at the age of about 16. Rimsky, a formidable teacher, was to be a key figure in Stravinsky's musical development, but – perhaps mindful of the snub he had received at the hands of Glazunov – it was not until some years later that the young composer plucked up the courage to approach him for advice.

The more Stravinsky's inner life came to focus itself on music – and a photograph of 1898 shows the walls of his room bedecked with portraits of the great composers – the more his external circumstances chafed him. He attended the Second St Petersburg Gymnasium, a government school, until the age of 15, getting up at seven o'clock in the morning for the long walk to his classes. He had few close friends there, and found a sympathetic teacher only in a Father Rojdestvensky, whose Bible studies instilled in him an enduring love of Slavonic.

The curriculum was heavily geared towards languages – a valuable grounding for a composer who was to spend most of his life in exile – and was no doubt influential in developing his obsession with etymology. (In adulthood, he would switch between languages at the drop of a hat, delighting in inter-lingual puns and interrupting conversations for half an hour at a time while he searched for derivations in his huge collection of dictionaries.) But for the most part, Stravinsky appears to have found school no more congenial than home. Meals were inedible – it is a reminder of the political ferment of the times that strikes were organised by the pupils in protest – and he was always hungry. He was also ribbed about his height, his diminutive stature being a source of surprise to many who met him in later life. Above all, he felt there was little common ground between himself and his peers. Tellingly, when he broke to his classmates the (to him) shattering news that Tchaikovsky was dead, one of them asked what grade he had been in.

His second school, to which he graduated in 1897, was a private one, the Gourévitch Gymnasium, which his brother Yury had also attended. Here the curriculum followed the classical model – history, Latin, Greek, Russian and French literature, mathematics – but the young Stravinsky's main pleasure lay in the eight-mile journey there and back, especially in winter when he would be driven along the Nevsky Prospect in a sleigh, protected by a net from the snow kicked up by the horse. Again, there was one congenial teacher, an ex-Hussar who taught mathematics and apparently encouraged his young charge to compose. Otherwise, it was the same story of dissatisfaction and rebelliousness: 'I was of course a very bad pupil,' Stravinsky was to recall, 'and I hated this school as I did all my schools, profoundly and forever.'

In 1901, at the instigation of his parents, he began a four-year law degree at St Petersburg University. Again, it is little surprise to learn from his own account that he was an indifferent student and attended only some 50 lectures during the whole of his time there; for by the end of his first year, two events had served irrevocably to determine the future course of his life.

The first was an indirect result of his university studies. One of his fellow students was Vladimir Rimsky-Korsakov, the youngest son of the composer and a competent violinist, and Stravinsky was soon on friendly terms with him. In the summer of 1902, Igor went with his parents to Bad Wildungen, a stone's throw from Heidelberg, where another of Rimsky's sons was at university. Rimsky was spending the summer with his own family at nearby Neckargemünd, and during the course of the vacation Vladimir invited his fellow-student to stay with them. In what was to prove the most important encounter of his life so far, Igor took the opportunity of this visit to consult Rimsky about his musical future.

He told the older musician of his own ambition to become a composer, and at his request played him some of his compositions – short piano pieces which may have included the 1902 *Scherzo* in G minor, a somewhat anodyne work and one of only three small pieces to have survived from Stravinsky's juvenilia. Rimsky's reaction was initially discouraging, but he seems nonetheless to have recognised Stravinsky's seriousness of purpose. He advised him to carry on with his university course, but at the same time to continue his private studies in harmony and counterpoint. Significantly, he also advised him against entering the Conservatoire, where he was himself a professor, intuiting, if Stravinsky's account is to be taken at face value, that he would be unsuited to the institutional régime and that, since he was already 20 years old, he might have a lot of catching up to do to. Most important of all, he added that Stravinsky could always go to him for advice and that he would be prepared to give him private lessons once he'd progressed a little further.

The interview was decisive for Stravinsky's future. Rimsky could be brutally frank in his musical judgements – on learning that one young aspirant composer was a doctor, he said simply 'Excellent. Continue to practise medicine' – and Stravinsky read his advice as a vote of confidence in his potential. Never slow to cultivate a useful connection, he was soon a regular at the weekly musical gatherings Rimsky held at his St Petersburg house, and he applied himself to his musical studies with renewed enthusiasm.

A few months after their summer discussion, another momentous event was to cement Stravinsky's relations with the Rimsky-Korsakov family and mark a final break with the past. Fyodor Stravinsky, who had been seriously ill for some time with cancer of the throat, died in December 1902. 'His death brought us close together,' said Stravinsky, cryptically. But it also represented an end to the 'time of humiliations'. From that moment on, Rimsky was to become not only an invaluable source of advice and, in due course, a formal teacher; he was also gradually to assume, at least in Stravinsky's mind, the role of an adoptive father.

Chapter 2

The years of apprenticeship (1903-1909)

In his *Memories and Commentaries,* Stravinsky said he had written nothing before his father's death. It was only a slight exaggeration. As we have seen, three pieces survive from the years 1898 to 1902 – a *Tarantella* for piano (1898), a Pushkin song 'Storm cloud' and the *Scherzo* for piano (both 1902) – and there were clearly others in the portfolio he presented to Rimsky-Korsakov at Neckargemünd. But it is a meagre output for a 20-year-old who claimed to feel a God-given calling for composition. Indeed, one cannot but wonder whether Rimsky was influenced more by ties of friendship to the Stravinsky family than by his proverbially dispassionate judgement in offering the young man his help at all. Certainly there was nothing in Stravinsky's bottom drawer to suggest the flair of Rimsky's former pupil Glazunov, who had taken St Petersburg by storm with his first symphony at the age of 16, or his future one Prokofiev, who had recently, at nine, completed his first opera. To all intents and purposes, as 1903 dawned, Stravinsky was still an absolute novice.

It is clear, though, that he was now determined to strike out along his own chosen path. Shortly after Fyodor's death, he made an abortive attempt at independence when he left home and went to live with one of his Yelachich cousins, only to be forced back to the Krukov Canal apartment shortly afterwards when his mother apparently feigned a serious illness. Of more significance, though, is the fact that by March 1903 there are reports of him playing his own compositions at Rimsky's weekly musical gatherings.

Most significantly of all, it was in the summer of 1903 that he began his first large-scale work – a piano sonata. This was the occasion of his second visit to his Uncle Yelachich's estate at Pavolvka, and his companion on the idyllic four-day boat trip along the Volga was Rimsky-Korsakov's son Vladimir. The two young men relished the riverside sights – the blue and gold churches of Jaroslav, the mendicant monks at Nishni-Novgorod, the booths selling mare's milk – and they sent postcards to Rimsky from every stage of the journey. At Pavlovka, however, Igor realised he had bitten off more than he could chew in attempting so ambitious a composition. He soon ran into formal difficulties and towards the end of the summer decided to take Rimsky up on his offer of advice. He accordingly made his way to Lzy, a village 100 miles south-east of St Petersburg where Rimsky had a summer house. Here he stayed with the Rimsky-Korsakov family for two weeks, during which time the older composer supplemented his hospitality with a crash course in sonata principles and set him to work on a sonatina to put them into practice. In the autumn, back in St Petersburg, Stravinsky started the formal lessons with Rimsky which were to last for the next three years. They were also to provide the grounding for his remarkable transformation, in the course of a single decade, from the gentleman dilettante of the last years of the nineteenth century to one of the most celebrated new composers of the twentieth.

At 59, Nikolay Rimsky-Korsakov was something of an institution in Russian musical life. An imposing and aristocratic figure, tall and bespectacled with a cascading beard, he was one of three surviving members of 'the Five' (or 'the mighty handful'), the group of so-called 'nationalist' composers who dominated the Russian musical scene in the second half of the nineteenth century (the other four being Mily Balakirev (1837-1910), Alexander Borodin (1833-87), César Cui (1835-1918) and Modest Mussorgsky (1839-81)). Today known chiefly for his symphonic suite *Sheherazade* and for the orchestral interlude 'The Flight of the Bumblebee' from his opera *The Legend of Tsar Saltan,* in turn-of-the-century St Petersburg Rimsky was fêted as an operatic composer and master of orchestral colour and was widely regarded as the greatest teacher of his generation. In 1871, when still a naval lieutenant with no formal musical training of his own, he was a surprise appointee as professor of composition at the recently founded St Petersburg Conservatoire and had held the post ever since. Far from a conventional establishment figure, however, he combined musical conservatism with liberal anti-Tsarist politics, and would be temporarily suspended from his professorship in 1905 for his support of revolutionary students. While provoking the exasperation of musical progressives such as Debussy, he inspired the affection of his many pupils,

'I am grateful to Rimsky for many things': Stravinsky's most influential teacher, Nikolay Rimsky-Korsakov (1844-1908)

one of whom, Stravinsky's future mentor Diaghilev, described him as embodying 'that good-natured mixture of schoolboy and schoolmaster which had always made us both laugh at and love him'.

Between 1903 and 1906 Stravinsky had lessons with Rimsky twice a week. These lasted a little over an hour and focused on orchestration. Rimsky would set him Beethoven piano sonatas or Schubert quartets and marches to orchestrate. He also gave him parts of the piano score of his newly completed opera *Pan Voyevoda* and would compare his pupil's orchestrations with his own, exploring the reasons for their different solutions. He was, by Stravinsky's account, a strict but patient teacher with remarkable powers of explanation, and the new pupil found his tuition 'unforgettable'. At the same time, having now apparently ditched Kalafaty, he continued his studies in harmony and counterpoint under his own steam, teaching himself as Rimsky too had done in his earlier years.

In addition to attending his formal lessons, Stravinsky claimed to have been at Rimsky's house every day for much of this period. This provided him with opportunities to meet many of the key musical figures of the time, since Rimsky's residence was a stop on the itinerary of most visiting musicians. Among those the young Stravinsky was introduced to in this way were the conductors Hans Richter and Arthur Nikisch, the conductor (and later Stravinsky's publisher) Serge Koussevitzky, and the composers Max Reger and Alexander Scriabin.

The conductor and publisher Serge Koussevitzky (1874-1951), who went on to première a number of Stravinsky's works

Stravinsky's writings paint a vivid picture of the factionalism of Russian musical life at this time. In particular, he describes the rivalry between the 'nationalist' Rimsky and the 'Westernising' Tchaikovsky schools of Russian music as a 'cold war'. (Stravinsky's own loyalties were divided while he remained Rimsky's pupil; only later would he declare himself of the Tchaikovsky camp, comparing the latter's freshness with the 'stale naturalism and amateurism of the "Five"'.) He has also left us a series of Aubreyesque pen-portraits of the leading musicians of their day, such as the aged Cui ('He was said to be an authority on fortifications. Indeed, I suspect he knew more about them than about counterpoint'); Anatol Lyadov ('... a darling man, as sweet and charming as his own *Musical Snuff Box*'); and Scriabin (whom Rimsky called 'the narcissus' and of whose music, according to Stravinsky, he once remarked "mais c'est du Rubinstein" ("Anton Rubinstein" being at this time a term of abuse equivalent to *merde*)').

The musical life of St Petersburg provided rich opportunities for a young musician determined to master his craft. For Stravinsky's generation, the cornerstones of its public music-making were two concert series: the so-called Evenings of Contemporary Music, organised by his friend and later 'co-autobiographer' Walter Nouvel; and the Russian Symphony Concerts, organised by the influential music publisher Belyayev. Not only did these concerts serve to widen Stravinsky's musical knowledge – the former series (despite its title!) giving him his first taste of Monteverdi and other pre-Baroque composers, as well as works by Debussy, Ravel, Dukas and d'Indy; they were also in due course to introduce the wider public to his own first compositions. They were significant too as a meeting-place for St Petersburg's young musicians, writers and artists, including Stravinsky's friends Ivan Pokrovsky and the writer and musician Stepan Mitusov. Mitusov in particular was an important new figure in Stravinsky's life. A fellow-member of Rimsky's circle – he and Stravinsky danced a cakewalk together at one of Rimsky's musical gatherings in February 1904 – he was well-versed in the artistic movements of Paris and Berlin and would later work with the composer on the libretto of *The Nightingale*, which is dedicated to him.

It was against this background of new musical experiences and friendships that Stravinsky continued to work on his sonata during 1904. He was also composing other piano pieces which he performed at Rimsky's weekly gatherings but which are now lost, as is the celebratory cantata he apparently wrote for his teacher's sixtieth birthday in March. An unpublished song for bass and piano – 'The Mushrooms Going to War' – also dates from this year.

On 22 February 1905, Stravinsky's *Sonata in F Sharp Minor* was given its first private performance before members of Rimsky-Korsakov's circle by the pianist Nicholas Richter, to whom it is dedicated. Richter also gave its public première at one of the Evenings of Contemporary Music. It was the first time a work of Stravinsky's had been heard in public.

Stravinsky believed the sonata had been lost – it was actually filed away in Leningrad's State Public Library, to be published in its first, Soviet edition only in 1973, two years after the composer's death – but he remembered it as 'an inept imitation of late Beethoven'. The remark is illuminating principally as a warning against taking Stravinsky's memories of his lost works at face value. The sonata in fact sits squarely within the Russian romantic tradition. Written in close consultation with Rimsky, it is a student work through and through, its thematic ideas at once full-blooded and curiously disjointed. In particular, the main theme of the finale, with its mixture of banality and bombast, seems quite unequal to the rhetorical weight it is required to bear, and the work leaves an uneasy impression of structural gestures too grandiose for its content. As his first essay in an extended classical form, however, it was a significant excursion into new musical territory for the 23-year-old composer and a marked advance on the miniatures with which he had regaled Rimsky at their initial interview.

It is perhaps an indication of how completely Stravinsky was now absorbed in music that one gets little sense from his reminiscences of the turmoil of life in St Petersburg during this period. If there was a year when the political tide in Russia turned irreversibly towards revolution it was 1905. While he was putting the finishing touches to the *Sonata*, the imperial forces had been suffering humiliating defeats in the Russo-Japanese War and dissatisfaction with the Tsar's leadership was rapidly spreading. In the countryside, peasants were rising up against their landlords. In the cities, students were rioting and industrial workers forming the first soviets to represent their interests. In January, only weeks before the *Sonata*'s first performance, St Petersburg was paralysed by strike action, and on what has become known as 'Bloody Sunday' troops opened fire on a vast demonstration of workers who were marching peacefully on the Winter Palace in the hope of having their grievances heard by Nicholas II – a shock to the Tsar's paternalistic image from which the régime was never

A rally of militant students at the University Building, St Petersburg, during Stravinsky's final year there, 1905

ultimately to recover. In the summer came news from Odessa of the mutiny of troops on the battleship *Potemkin*, immortalised in Eisenstein's seminal film.

It was amid these revolutionary tensions that in May of 1905 Stravinsky finished his law studies at St Petersburg University, thus setting the formal seal on a phase of his life which had closed in all but externals in 1902. He later claimed to recall only two incidents of any moment related to his university career, both from this final year. The first concerned his final examinations, when, fearing he would fail one paper, he swapped identities and exams with a fellow-student, whose strong subject matched Stravinsky's weak one and *vice versa* – a deception which appears to have been successful, since Stravinsky was duly issued with a certificate of graduation. The second incident was a direct result of the social upheavals of the times and one of the very few occasions when they seem to have touched him personally. One afternoon, he was walking through the Kazansky Place when he became caught up in a student demonstration and was arrested by the police. He was released without charge, but the terror of his seven-hour detention never left him.

Immediately after leaving university, Stravinsky took a holiday in Scandinavia with his brother Gury, staying briefly in Helsingfors with an uncle who was the civil governor of Finland, and catching a treasured glimpse of Ibsen in the street in Oslo. At the end of the summer he had some difficulty in returning to St Petersburg because of strike action by workers in the transport and other key industries. At about the same time, under Rimsky's watchful eye, he began work on his first orchestral composition, the *Symphony in E Flat Major.*

In the autumn of 1905, Stravinsky announced his engagement to his cousin Catherine Nossyenko, to whom he had been deeply attached since their childhood games at Pechisky in the summers of the early 1890s. 'From our first hour together' he wrote in *Expositions and Developments,*

'we both seemed to realize that we would one day marry – or so we told each other later. Perhaps we were always more like brother and sister. I was a deeply lonely child, and I wanted a sister of my own. Catherine… came into my life as a kind of long-wanted sister in my tenth year. We were from then until her death extremely close, and closer than lovers sometimes are, for mere lovers may be strangers though they live and love together all their lives.'

Catherine and Igor Stravinsky
in 1907

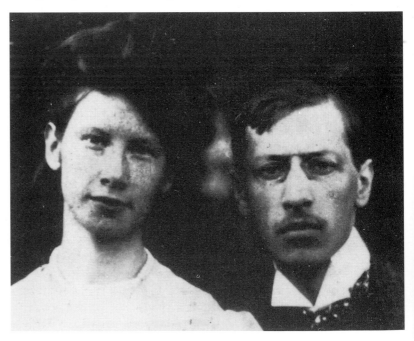

In addition to her selflessness and kindness, of which her surviving letters to Stravinsky are a remarkable witness, Catherine's interest in music must also have been an important factor in their closeness. She had spent much of the last three years in Paris, studying drawing and singing, and had an attractive soprano voice. She was a sufficiently accomplished pianist to play Beethoven symphonies in four-handed piano arrangements with her husband, and was also a skilled music copyist, in which capacity Stravinsky was increasingly to rely on her as the years went by. Just as their relationship had outlasted the more passionate attachments of Igor's adolescence, so the marriage was to survive his infidelity and the demands of fame, ending only with Catherine's death from tuberculosis 34 years later.

The wedding itself took place in January 1906 in the village of Novaya Derevnya, just outside St Petersburg. It was a secretive affair, since marriage between first cousins was forbidden by imperial decree; the only witnesses were Rimsky's sons Andrey and Vladimir, who held the gold and velvet wedding crown over the couple's heads. Rimsky himself was waiting for them with an icon and a blessing when they got home, and made them a wedding present of his teaching, for which he seems anyway not to have charged Stravinsky before. The newly-weds then left from the Finland Station for Imatra, a popular honeymoon resort which Stravinsky described as a sort of Finnish Niagara. It was during their two-week stay that he had his first musical ideas for the song-suite which was to become *The Faun and the Shepherdess (Faune et bergère)*. Back in St Petersburg, the couple moved in with his mother, taking over two rooms of the Krukov Canal flat – an arrangement which could hardly have been the most comfortable start to their married life. It was also at around this time that they paid a visit of respect to Glinka's aged sister, Lyudmila Shestakova, who had been a friend of Stravinsky's father and who seems, to judge by Diaghilev's account of worshipping at the same shrine some years earlier, to have become something of an object of pilgrimage for Russian music lovers.

In February of the following year, 1907, Igor and Catherine's first child, Theodore, was born and they moved to their own flat on the English Prospect, which was to be their base until 1910. Stravinsky was also having a house built to his own plans on the banks of the River Luga at Ustilug, where the couple had chosen to spend their summers. Not only was this country retreat to prove a congenial place for composing (Stravinsky soon moved his grand piano there from St Petersburg); it was also the centre of an extensive estate, the management of which took up a great deal of Stravinsky's time and provided him with a very comfortable income.

In May, Rimsky arranged for Stravinsky to hear the two middle movements of his work-in-progress, the *Symphony in E Flat Major*, in a private performance by the court orchestra under H Wahrlich, the imperial Kapellmeister (who conducted it in full military uniform). The work was affectionately dedicated to Rimsky, under whose close supervision it was written, and the master sat next to his pupil making critical remarks throughout the performance, especially about the heaviness of the orchestration, which, according to one of Stravinsky's accounts of the event, Glazunov also found fault with. Igor's Uncle Yelachich was in the audience and presented his nephew with a commemorative medal to mark the occasion; Rimsky himself made his pupil a gift of the manuscript score of *The Legend of Tsar Saltan*. The full symphony was given its first public performance at one of Belyayev's Russian Symphony Concerts at the beginning of 1908, under the baton of Felix Blumenfeld.

It is easy to see the *Symphony in E Flat* as merely a student exercise, but it is by any standards a work of remarkable assurance for someone whose compositions had thus far been limited to piano pieces and songs. There is a confidence in the handling of the orchestra – particularly in the gracefully bustling Scherzo, here placed second of the four movements – which Rimsky, for all his critical interventions, must surely have recognised as demonstrating a natural flair for the medium. Above all, it shows how thoroughly Stravinsky had assimilated his principal models – Glazunov, Tchaikovsky (whose strong presence in the slow movement must have given Rimsky pause for thought) and of course Rimsky himself. Stravinsky, always his own severest critic, seems to have retained a soft spot for his Opus 1, telling one of the journalists who besieged him after the successes of *The Firebird* and *Petrushka* that for all its faults he was not at all ashamed of it. He continued to tinker with it over the years and in 1966 included it as part of his landmark series of recordings for Columbia Records. He would hardly have disagreed, though, with Rimsky's private assessment, as reported by one of his other pupils, that 'the talent of Igor Stravinsky has not yet taken clear shape'.

The same concert at which the *Symphony* was first performed may also have seen the première of *The Faun and the Shepherdess,* a suite of three short songs for mezzo soprano and orchestra on poems by Pushkin. Dedicated to his new wife Catherine, the songs – 'The Shepherdess', 'The Faun' and 'The Torrent' – tell, in an atmosphere of sensuality by turns languid and turbulent, the story of an adolescent girl discovering her love for a shepherd lad, but attracting the notice of a faun from whose lustful pursuit she escapes only by plunging to her death in a river. Stravinsky said that Rimsky found the first song strange, and the 'use of whole-tone progressions suspiciously "Debussy-ist"' – tendencies barely discernible in the music today. (But then Rimsky's attitude to Debussy was highly ambiguous. 'Better not listen to him,' Stravinsky reported him saying; 'one runs the risk of getting accustomed to him and one would end by liking him.')

Perhaps the best summary of the qualities of these compositions, his first large-scale pieces to reach an audience outside his immediate circle, is the one Stravinsky himself provided in his *Conversations*: 'I know that my first works, the *Faune et Bergère* and the *Symphony in E Flat,* lack personality while at the same time they demonstrate definite technical ability with the musical materials', he wrote, going on to say that they sound 'like Stravinsky... only through thickly bespectacled hindsight' – thus identifying precisely the perspective from which, like all his works before *The Firebird,* they have generally been viewed ever since.

Stravinsky's music was now beginning to be heard more frequently on the concert platform. In addition to the premières of the *Symphony* and *The Faun,* the 1907/1908 season of Evenings of Contemporary Music also saw the first performances of the *Pastorale,* a wordless vocalise for soprano and piano, and the two songs – 'Spring' and 'Song of the Dew' – to words by the poet Gorodyetsky, in which Stravinsky himself accompanied Elizabeth Petrenko at the keyboard. The *Pastorale,* of which Stravinsky later made arrangements for different combinations of instruments, is a delightful miniature written for Rimsky's daughter Nadyezhda, its melodic line meandering within strict limits like a stream within its banks. The Gorodyetsky songs, however, won the approval neither of Rimsky, who found both the words and music of 'Spring' too 'decadent' for his taste, nor of Gorodyetsky himself, who thought the long, slow bells of his poem reduced to 'a kind of jingle bells' by Stravinsky's piano writing.

In the summer of 1907 Stravinsky had begun a new orchestral showpiece, the *Scherzo fantastique,* and shortly afterwards also started work on the first act of an opera, *The Nightingale (Le Rossignol)* derived from the fairy stories of Hans Christian Andersen. The *Scherzo fantastique* seems loosely to have been based on Maeterlinck's philosophical work *La Vie des abeilles* – though a more detailed apiary programme was developed only for its performance as a ballet a decade later – and Stravinsky claimed later to have borrowed from Rimsky's 'Flight of the Bumblebee' in the composition, as he certainly also did from Wagner and Dukas. Rimsky spoke highly of the work, the manuscript of which Stravinsky sent him in the spring of 1908. It was to be the last he saw.

The same spring, Stravinsky told his teacher of his plans to compose another short orchestral work, *Fireworks (Feu d'artifice),* to mark the forthcoming marriage of Rimsky's daughter Nadyezhda to the composer Maximilian Steinberg. During six weeks at Ustilug in the summer, he completed the composition and sent it to Rimsky for his views. A few days later, he received a telegram informing him of Rimsky's death; the manuscript itself was returned shortly afterwards bearing the words 'Not delivered on account of death of addressee.' Stravinsky was stunned. 'Few people can have been as close to Rimsky as I was,' he was later to write, and he felt his death deeply. He broke down at the funeral, which he later described as one of the unhappiest days of his life. Rimsky's widow's tactless attempt to comfort him with the words 'Why so unhappy? We still have Glazunov', was, he said, the cruellest remark he ever heard; 'I have never hated again as I did that moment', he told Robert Craft in *Conversations.* Extreme though his reaction may appear, it was the beginning of an inexorable estrangement from the whole family.

We shall probably never know what Rimsky-Korsakov really thought of his most famous pupil. He certainly merited not a single mention in Rimsky's autobiography, and Stravinsky's claim that his silence was designed to avoid favouritism rings defensively hollow. Two among various pieces of anecdotal evidence suggest, though, that Rimsky recognised, even from the few less than characteristic works produced under his tutelage, that Stravinsky was a talent to be reckoned with. One comes from a correspondent of Stravinsky's in the 1920s, a former friend of Rimsky's, who recalled the latter saying: 'Igor Stravinsky may be my pupil, but he will never be my or anyone else's follower, because his gift for music is uniquely great and original.' Another comes from Diaghilev, whose unpublished memoirs (as translated by Richard Buckle in his compendious biography of the impresario) tell the story of Stravinsky showing his master a new composition. 'After reading through it, Rimsky burst out "This is disgusting, Sir. No, Sir, it is not permissible to write such nonsense until one is sixty." He was in a bad mood all day; then, at dinner, he exclaimed to his wife "What a herd of nonentities my pupils are! There's not one of them capable of producing a piece of rubbish such as Igor brought me this morning!'" Who knows, though, how compromised by Stravinsky's later fame these reminiscences may be.

Alexander Glazunov (1865-1936), whom Stravinsky described as one of the most disagreeable men he had ever met

Whatever Rimsky's view of his pupil, there can be no doubt that for Stravinsky the value of his teaching was immense. Stravinsky himself recognised this, however grudging some of his later acknowledgements of the fact. 'There is only one course for the beginner,' he wrote in his *Autobiography*: 'he must first accept a discipline imposed from without, but only as the means of obtaining freedom for, and strengthening himself in, his own method of expression.' Rimsky provided that discipline at a crucial moment in the young composer's development, and for that Stravinsky remained forever grateful to him.

The immediate expression of that gratitude was the *Chant funèbre* for wind instruments, which was performed at a memorial concert for Rimsky in the Grand Hall of the St Petersburg Conservatoire in February 1909. The manuscript of this piece was lost during the 1917 Revolution, but Stravinsky himself remembered it as the best of his works before *The Firebird*. In his *Autobiography* he described the idea behind it as a sort of tributary procession in which 'all the solo instruments of the orchestra filed past the tomb of the master in succession, each laying down its melody as its wreath against a deep background of tremolo murmurings simulating the vibrations of bass voices singing in chorus.' Both he and the audience were deeply moved by the occasion.

One can only surmise what Rimsky would have thought of Stravinsky's other composition of that summer, the *Four Studies* for piano Op. 7. The influence of the 'narcissus' Scriabin hangs over the work, as Stravinsky himself was later to acknowledge, but it perhaps requires less than usually bespectacled hindsight to see in the startlingly mechanical-sounding second study, with its subtly dislocated lines, an augur of the mature composer.

A week before the performance of the *Chant funèbre*, the *Scherzo fantastique* and *Fireworks* had been premièred at a concert in St Petersburg conducted by Alexander Ziloti. The audience included Glazunov, who was characteristically caustic about the new music – 'No talent, only dissonance' – and Stravinsky's friend Pierre Suvchinsky, who remembered the composer's aunt coming up to him afterwards and saying, not 'Congratulations' as everyone expected, but 'How is Mama?' Most significantly of all, the audience also included the great impresario Diaghilev.

The concert was to prove a key event in Stravinsky's unfolding career. The orchestral virtuosity of the *Scherzo fantastique* and, especially, of *Fireworks* – four minutes of appropriately pyrotechnic instrumental display, the suddenly calm central section of which includes a passage all but

Serge Diaghilev (1872-1929), whose partnership with Stravinsky was to change the course of twentieth-century music

plagiarised from Dukas' *The Sorcerer's Apprentice* – clearly made a favourable impression on Diaghilev, who was already filling his famous black notebooks with plans for his 1910 Paris season. Always on the look-out for new talent, he soon commissioned Stravinsky to provide the opening and closing numbers for *Les Sylphides,* a ballet based on music by Chopin which he was to stage in Paris in the summer of 1909. The first-fruits of what would prove one of the defining partnerships of twentieth-century music were thus two modest orchestrations of Chopin piano pieces, the *Nocturne* in A flat and the *Valse brillante* in E flat. (It used to be thought that Stravinsky's orchestration of *Kobold* from Grieg's *Lyric Pieces* was also made for the 1909 season, but it now seems more likely to have been written for the ballet *Les Orientales,* which was programmed with *The Firebird* in 1910.)

While *Les Sylphides* was being danced in Paris at the Théâtre du Châtelet in May, Stravinsky, in Ustilug, continued work on the first act of *The Nightingale*. Already in the background, though, was another commission which would change the whole course of his life. For the 1910 Paris season, Diaghilev planned to break with his usual practice of importing existing works in favour of creating a new ballet from scratch. At some stage during 1909 he commissioned Lyadov to write the music for a ballet to be called *The Firebird* – a title he was already using for one of the numbers (actually the *Bluebird pas de deux* from *The Sleeping Beauty*) in his 1909 ballet *Le Festin*. But Lyadov was a notoriously slow writer and it must soon have become clear to Diaghilev that he wasn't going to come up with the goods; indeed, the impresario had already discussed the ballet with Stravinsky. As a result, when in the final weeks of 1909 he telephoned the 27-year-old composer to ask him to take over the commission, the latter surprised him by saying that he had already started work on it.

At the end of 1902 Stravinsky had gone to Rimsky-Korsakov with a few undistinguished miniatures to show for his dreams of a composing career. A little over six years and a mere handful of works later, he was now on the verge of his first and perhaps his greatest international triumph.

Chapter 3

Celebrity (1910-1914)

Serge Diaghilev was a giant figure on the cultural stage in the years before the First World War. Editor, exhibition-organiser, concert-promoter, patron – the word 'impresario' barely does justice to the extraordinary range of his interests and activities. A tireless organiser, by the time he commissioned *The Firebird* from Stravinsky at the age of 38 he already had to his credit the editorship of the short-lived but hugely influential art journal *The World of Art* (*Mir Isskustva*); a series of major exhibitions, including one which brought the work of Russian artists to the Grand Palais in Paris in 1906; and three seasons of musical triumphs in the French capital, at which he had introduced to the Parisian public such luminaries of Russian musical life as Rachmaninov, the great dramatic bass Chaliapin and, most memorably of all, the leading lights of the Russian ballet. An assiduous cultivator of influential connections in artistic and aristocratic circles, he had friends at the Russian court, had taken tea with Tolstoy and had walked arm-in-arm through Paris with the exiled Oscar Wilde.

Above all, as his successful 1909 Paris season once again demonstrated, Diaghilev had a keen instinct for what would make an impression (if not always a profit) in the theatre. He also had the sheer tenacity of purpose to bring it to the stage. Cajoling, bullying and charming, he would never take no for an answer, firing off telegrams from every stage of his bewilderingly convoluted travels, descending on associates at the drop of a hat to argue his case in person, or summoning them halfway across Europe for a conversation. At the time when his career first became harnessed to Stravinsky's, his entourage already included the artists Alexandre Benois and Léon Bakst, the revolutionary choreographer Mikhail Fokine and the young dancers Anna Pavlova, Tamara Karsavina and Vaslav Nijinsky, with whom he was involved in an obsessive affair. A glittering constellation of talent, it was

Diaghilev and friends

also a hotbed of political and sexual intrigue, perpetually on the verge of disintegration.

Stravinsky was later to say that he and Diaghilev understood each other from the first day. Certainly, they had a great deal in common. They had both studied law at St Petersburg University and music with Rimsky-Korsakov, whose version of Mussorgsky's opera *Boris Godunov* Diaghilev had presented during his 1908 Paris season. They may even have been distant cousins. Biographers of both men have noted their constitutional hatred of self-repetition, which was to become such a hallmark of Stravinsky's musical development. The composer also shared with his new mentor a genuine love of musical theatre in general and of ballet in particular, and launched himself into learning the ropes with characteristic single-mindedness. Newly released from the formalism of Rimsky's musical world, he relished the ferment of creativity in which the Ballets Russes circle lived, and their ardour for the experimental both stimulated and reacted with his own. Diaghilev's commissioning of Stravinsky was itself an example of that willingness to risk the new: after all, in 1909 the young St Petersburger was still virtually unknown.

This, then, was the heady atmosphere in which Stravinsky now found himself working. And work he certainly did. The première of *The Firebird* (*L'Oiseau de feu*) was scheduled for June 1910, which left barely six months for the work to be composed, choreographed, costumed, set, rehearsed and publicised – not to mention the myriad administrative demands of mounting a new ballet in a foreign capital. Stravinsky had never undertaken anything on this scale before, and his only experience of writing to a deadline had been the slender ballet

Rehearsing *The Firebird* in 1910:
Stravinsky (at the keyboard),
Fokine (leaning against the
piano) and Karsavina

orchestrations Diaghilev had commissioned from him for the previous year's season. Nonetheless, by March he had completed the work in short score, and the orchestral score was finished in all but details a month later.

Stravinsky worked closely with Fokine on the choreography, though exactly who did what would remain a source of contention between them for years to come. Stravinsky ranked Fokine with Glazunov as one of the most disagreeable men he had ever met, but he recognised superior experience when he met it, and admitted to learning a lot from their collaboration. Indeed, he used it as the model for all his later dealings with choreographers. He studied the libretto episode by episode and familiarised himself with 'the exact measurements required of the music', finding, not for the last time in his career, inspiration in exactitude and freedom in the constraints imposed by form and circumstance.

The première of *The Firebird* took place at the Paris Opera House on 25 June 1910. It was a triumph. Stravinsky remembered the glitter and perfume of the first-night audience and the procession of notables who passed through Diaghilev's box during the intermissions. At the end of the performance, he took numerous curtain calls. He was still on stage after the final curtain had descended when he saw coming towards him Diaghilev and 'a dark man with a double forehead whom he introduced as Claude Debussy'. The older composer complimented the younger on his music and invited him to dinner. It was the beginning of a friendship which was to continue, albeit not without professional jealousies, for the remaining years of Debussy's life.

It is difficult for the modern listener to recapture the force of the impression made by *The Firebird* on those first audiences. The exoticism of the story has faded with time, and its protagonists – the firebird herself (danced by Karsavina at the première), the handsome young prince Ivan Tsarevich, and the evil monster Kashchei, who holds virgins captive and turns would-be rescuers to stone – seem too like stock types from the pantomime to lift it into universality. The music remains a dazzling accomplishment, of an order barely heralded in Stravinsky's previous compositions. The huge orchestral palette and the subtle mastery with which Stravinsky deploys it to illuminate characters and situations are both phenomenal; the natural-harmonic string glissando in the 'Introduction' is only the most conspicuous of the novel instrumental effects which attracted notice and admiration from the first. But it is easier today than it was in 1910 to see that, for all its virtuosity,

With Debussy at his home in avenue du Bois de Boulogne, 1910

The Firebird belongs as much to the nineteenth century as to the twentieth. Even so ostensibly 'modern' a number as the 'Infernal Dance of all Kashchei's Subjects' has more in common with Rimsky's orchestration of Mussorgsky's *Night on the Bare Mountain* than with the explosive assymetries of *The Rite of Spring*. Similarly, the 'General Thanksgiving' with which the ballet ends contains more than an echo of Mussorgsky's 'Great Gate of Kiev'. The music outperforms Rimsky on his home ground, but for all its brilliance it is not yet characteristically Stravinskyan. In later years, the composer claimed to have become dissatisfied with the score even as he was writing it, describing the orchestral forces as 'wastefully large' and the music as lacking in originality. Indeed, soon after its initial run he set about quarrying from it the first of the three concert suites which he regarded as successive criticisms of the original and which have assured the work a popular place in the repertoire ever since. That popularity – something of a double-edged sword for a composer whose musical language was now evolving so rapidly – was such that decades later he would be addressed in all seriousness by one American celebrity-spotter as 'Mr Fireberg'!

If *The Firebird* falls short of being a turning point in Stravinsky's musical development – a role reserved for his next great ballet, *Petrushka* – it was certainly a turning point in his career. After the first performances, like Byron after *Childe Harold*, he woke to find himself famous. Journalists jockeyed to interview him, popular portraitists to add him to their portfolios. Observers began to record his appearance, manner and table-talk. Debussy was only the first of many eminent and not so eminent figures to beat a path to the young man's door. The salons of Paris were suddenly open to him, and in the coming months he would make the acquaintance of a wide spectrum of artists, writers and musicians, including Maurice Ravel, Manuel de Falla, Marcel Proust, Jean Cocteau and Saint-John Perse. While Stravinsky's new-found celebrity opened up new friendships, however, it also placed a strain on old ones. *The Firebird* is dedicated to Andrey Rimsky-Korsakov, who was often with Stravinsky during its composition, but its success seems to have caused another deterioration in relations with the Rimsky-Korsakov family, who perhaps saw his independent path as an implied slur on the memory of their paterfamilias.

But Stravinsky had little time to consider such side-effects of his sudden fame. In July, he returned to Ustilug to collect his wife and children (Theodore now had a two-year-old sister, Lyudmila, known as 'Mika') and took Catherine, who was heavily pregnant again, to hear the final performance of *The Firebird* at the Opéra. He then accompanied them to the seaside in Brittany for a much-needed rest. It was during this short holiday that he set the *Two Poems of Verlaine* for baritone and piano, Op. 9 (the last composition to which he gave an opus number). The songs were dedicated to Gury, and it was a source of lasting regret to Stravinsky that his brother died before he had a chance to sing them professionally. But a new and much larger work had already seeded itself in his mind. In his *Autobiography* he described the now famous moment of inspiration:

'One day, when I was finishing the last pages of *L'Oiseau de Feu* in St Petersburg, I had a fleeting vision which came to me as a complete surprise, my mind at the moment being full of other things. I saw in imagination a solemn pagan rite: sage elders, seated in a circle, watched a young girl dance herself to death. They were sacrificing her to propitiate the god of spring.'

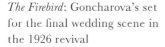

The Firebird: Goncharova's set for the final wedding scene in the 1926 revival

Such was the genesis of *The Rite of Spring* (*Le Sacre du printemps*). Stravinsky discussed the new work, soon provisionally titled 'The Great Sacrifice', with his friend, the Russian painter Nicolas Roerich, whose ethnological expertise was to be crucial in determining its final shape. There is a conspiratorial tone to the correspondence with Roerich which suggests that they wanted to keep the idea to themselves as long as possible, but with Diaghilev hungry for a new ballet to

47

Tamara Karsavina (1885-1978)
as the Firebird

consolidate the success of *The Firebird*, Stravinsky knew they'd have to tell him, and they did.

In the meantime, yet another work had seized his imagination. 'Before tackling the *Sacre du printemps*,' he wrote in his *Autobiography*, '... I wanted to refresh myself by composing an orchestral piece in which the piano would play the most important part – a sort of *Konzertstück*. In composing the music, I had in mind a distinct picture of a puppet, suddenly endowed with life, exasperating the patience of the orchestra with diabolical cascades of arpeggios.' The concertante element was soon diluted, but the underlying idea remained. Thus, in the first weeks after *The Firebird*, *Petrushka* too was conceived.

In August, while Stravinsky was making the first sketches for *The Rite* and starting work on *Petrushka*, the family moved to Chardon Jogny, near Vevey in Switzerland, and from there decamped to Lausanne, where their third child, a boy, Soulima, was born in September. Stravinsky himself lived in the clinic with Catherine after her confinement, but also rented an attic across the road for writing. It was here that Diaghilev and Nijinsky visited him to find out how *The Rite* was coming along and were surprised to find him working on a different piece altogether. When Stravinsky played them what he had already written, they were captivated. Diaghilev, with his customary eye for theatrical possibilities, saw in it just the ballet he needed for his 1911 season, which was the first to feature the Ballets Russes as a permanent company rather than an *ad hoc* ensemble of dancers. Once Catherine had recovered, the family moved to the Hôtel Châtelard in Clarens, the town on Lake Geneva which was to be their base of operations for most of the next four years, and it was there, while walking along the quay one day, that Stravinsky hit on the title *Petrushka* for the new composition. The majority of the work on the ballet was done at Beaulieu-sur-mer, near Nice, where the Stravinskys moved for the winter.

Meanwhile, Diaghilev had conscripted his old friend, the painter Alexandre Benois, to collaborate on the designs and the scenario. Stravinsky found Benois a far more congenial partner than Fokine, with whom nonetheless he worked on the choreography, and the two men got on well. The dynamics of the project were different from the outset, though. This time it was Stravinsky himself who was in the driving seat. Benois and Fokine heard the music for the first time at Christmas, when Stravinsky played through what he had written during a seasonal visit to St Petersburg. It was a quick trip, largely a duty call to his mother, but it served to refresh the composition of

Alexandre Benois (1870-1960), who designed the first *Petrushka*. Portrait by Léon Bakst

Petrushka with some first-hand exposure to the realities of Russian urban life. At the same time, Stravinsky found St Petersburg small and provincial in comparison with the Paris of his recent experience. It was a sadly mixed impression to take away from a city which, in the event, he was not to see again for more than half a century.

Back in Beaulieu, with his deadline looming, Stravinsky was suddenly struck down by one of the many illnesses which were to punctuate the coming years. In this case it was intercostal neuralgia, brought on, it seems, by nicotine poisoning. The smoking habit he had fed in his teenage years backstage at the Mariinsky had caught up with him – he dreamt he had become a hunchback and woke to find it almost true – and it was months before he regained his strength. Nonetheless, in May he was able to travel to Rome to meet Diaghilev and his company, who were performing there during the International Exhibition, and by the end of the month the new score was complete. This left only a month for rehearsals before the première, which took place at the Théâtre du Châtelet in Paris on 13 June under the baton of the 36-year-old Pierre Monteux. Despite the rush, and rather to Stravinsky's surprise, *Petrushka* was another triumph.

The ballet is in four scenes and tells the story of the eponymous puppet. The first scene is set at the Shrovetide Fair in St Petersburg and the music conveys with an almost cinematic sweep the bustle and activity of the crowds and the performances of dancers and street musicians. Suddenly a Showman appears, displaying three puppets in his theatre-booth: Petrushka, the Blackamoor and the Ballerina. He charms them to life with his flute in an episode known as the *Tour de passe-passe* – the 'sonorous magic' of which was greatly admired by Debussy – and they dance for the crowd. The second scene is set in Petrushka's cell, where Petrushka, now experiencing human emotions, curses his ugliness and isolation; he is visited and rejected by the Ballerina, with whom he has fallen in love. The third scene takes place in the Blackamoor's cell, where Stravinsky's sinister music evokes the Blackamoor's tiger-like pacing. The Ballerina visits him too and falls in love; in an episode based on two Viennese waltzes by Joseph Lanner, the two puppets dance together. Petrushka bursts in but the Blackamoor throws him out. The final scene returns to the Shrovetide Fair. It is now evening and out of the milling crowds crystallise the dances of wet-nurses, a peasant leading a bear, gypsies, coachmen and masqueraders. Suddenly Petrushka appears, pursued by the Blackamoor, who strikes

Clockwise from top left: The
most exciting human being
Stravinsky had ever seen on
stage: Nijinsky as Petrushka.
Court coachman and nurse:
Benois' costume designs for
Petrushka. Petrushka's cell:
Benois' stage design for the
second tableau of the ballet.
The Shrovetide Fair: Benois'
stage design for the first
tableau of *Petrushka*

51

him down and leaves him to die in the gently falling snow. As the crowd thins out and the Showman drags the stricken puppet away, Petrushka's ghost – which Stravinsky conceived as the 'real' Petrushka – pops up on the roof of the theatre-booth, thumbing his nose at the audience to the derisive trumpet arpeggios of the famous 'Petrushka chord'.

Not all of this, which is a mixture of Stravinsky's and his collaborators' ideas, was conveyed in Fokine's original choreography. Stravinsky was particularly critical of Fokine's failure to convey the insulting nature of Petrushka's final gesture, but he acknowledged the solo and ensemble dances of the framing tableaux as Fokine's greatest achievement. Above all, he was overwhelmed, as were many observers, including the wheelchair-bound Sarah Bernhardt, by the sheer force of Nijinsky's performance in the title role. As Petrushka, he recalled many years later, Nijinsky was quite simply the most exciting human being he had ever seen on a stage.

Stravinsky's musical language was to change often over the years, but in *Petrushka* he found for the first time his authentic voice. There are numerous borrowings in the work – the Lanner waltzes, an assortment of Russian folk and street songs – but all are transformed and subsumed into the greater musical architecture by his idiosyncratic touch. (One, the music-hall song *'Elle avait un'jambe en bois'*, was soon to cause him legal difficulties. He'd picked it up from the hurdy-gurdy which played under his window at Beaulieu and had assumed it to be traditional; in fact, it was still in copyright.) If some of its elements were familiar enough – Russian folk music was, after all, a staple of Rimsky's own vocabulary – the originality of the work as a whole was widely recognised. Stravinsky himself later described it as an implied criticism of 'the Five', and it certainly widened still further the rift between him and the Rimsky-Korsakov family; Andrey went so far as to damn it in a newspaper review as 'Russian vodka with French perfumes'. For many progressive musicians, however, it was cause for celebration, and at a lunch shortly after the first performance Debussy made Stravinsky a present of a walking stick with an inscribed monogram of their joint initials. The success of *The Firebird* was more than consolidated. As one London newspaper wrote after the English première of *Petrushka* in February 1913, 'the young composer of this extraordinary music stands before Europe as one of the most important figures in his profession'.

Stravinsky himself was more laconic. 'The success of *Petroushka* was good for me,' he wrote in *Expositions and Developments*, 'in that it gave me the absolute conviction of my

Nicolas Roerich (1874-1947), Stravinsky's collaborator on the scenario for *The Rite of Spring*

ear just as I was about to begin *Le Sacre du printemps*.' And it was to *The Rite of Spring* that he now immediately turned. In July, only weeks after the première of *Petrushka*, he travelled to Princess Tenisheva's estate near Smolensk – sharing a railway cattle-car with a none too accommodating bull! – to plan out the scenario with Roerich. In August, he visited Diaghilev in Karlsbad, where the work was formally commissioned, then made his way, with social and business stops in Warsaw, Lugano and Berlin, to Ustilug. Here he composed the two short songs for high voice and piano on lyrics by the Russian poet Balmont – 'The Forget-me-not' and 'The Dove' – and the strange six-minute cantata for male-voice choir and orchestra, *Zvezdoliki*. The latter work, the title of which can be literally translated as

'Starface' but is usually more elegantly rendered as *Le Roi des étoiles*, also sets words by Balmont. The poem is an apocalyptic vision some way after *Revelations*, but Stravinsky seems to have been untroubled by its impenetrability. '*Zvezdoliki* is obscure as poetry and as mysticism,' he later wrote, 'but its words are good, and words were what I needed, not meanings.' The statement is characteristic of Stravinsky's attitude to texts throughout his career. 'When I work with words in music,' he wrote in *Dialogues*, 'my musical saliva is set in motion by the sounds and rhythms of the syllables, and "In the beginning was the word" is, for me, a literal, localized truth.' *Zvezdoliki* was dedicated to Debussy, who called it a 'cantata for planets' and predicted that it would prove unperformable. In old age, Stravinsky called it his most 'difficult' composition, and though the comment says as much about his taste for controversial hyperbole as it does about the music, *Zvezdoliki* certainly remains one of his least played works, receiving its first performance only in 1939.

Monumental though its aspirations are, *Zvezdoliki* has little in common with Stravinsky's other large-scale undertaking of the summer of 1911. For it was at Ustilug too that he began serious work on *The Rite of Spring*, continuing it in great excitement at Clarens when the family returned there for the winter. They had now left the Hôtel Châtelard for a *pension* called Les Tilleuls (The Lindens), where they were to live until 1913. Here the majority of *The Rite* was written at a muted upright piano in a closet just eight feet square, while a village boy complained about the 'wrong notes' in the street outside. By January 1912 Stravinsky had completed Part One: 'The Adoration of the Earth'. In March, working on Part Two: 'The Sacrifice', he played what he had so far written to Diaghilev and Nijinsky during a visit to Monte Carlo and wrote to his mother that they were 'wild about it'. Back in Clarens he wrote enthusiastically to Roerich that he felt he had 'penetrated the secret of the rhythm of spring, and that musicians will feel it'. A week later, however, came the news that Diaghilev could not stage *The Rite* in 1912 after all because of unforeseen changes in the company's summer itinerary, and it would therefore be delayed to the 1913 season. Despite his disappointment, Stravinsky made good progress with the music, playing it to Diaghilev in Monte Carlo in April. Pierre Monteux, who was also present, described the composer stamping his feet and jumping up and down as he pounded away at the keyboard – one of many accounts of Stravinsky's alarmingly physical response to the rhythms of his work.

Meanwhile, Diaghilev, keen to promote his lover Nijinsky as a choreographer as well as a dancer, was planning to have him choreograph the new work instead of Fokine – a prospect the composer, who thought Nijinsky a musical illiterate, regarded with mixed feelings. In Paris in the summer, Stravinsky was in the audience when Nijinsky, testing his choreographic wings on Debussy's *L'Après-midi d'un faune*, caused a minor scandal by his portrayal of a sexual act at the climax of the piece. He also shared a box with Ravel at the première of the latter's ballet *Daphnis et Chloë*. The following day, 8 June, he played *The Rite* four-handed with Debussy in the presence of Louis Laloy, Debussy's friend and biographer. 'When they had finished,' Laloy recalled, 'there was no question of embracing, nor even of compliments. We were dumbfounded, overwhelmed by this hurricane which had come from the depths of the ages, and which had taken life by the roots.' Months later, the occasion still haunted Debussy 'like a beautiful nightmare'.

A few days afterwards, Stravinsky made his first visit to London for the English première of *The Firebird* and was presented to Queen Alexandra, whom he described as looking like a birthday cake. (Since she was quite deaf, he suspected she had not the slightest idea who he was or what he was doing in her box!) His summer itinerary also included Bayreuth, where a performance of *Parsifal* dispelled whatever was left of his adolescent crush on Wagner, and his first visit to Venice, where he played through *The Rite* for Diaghilev and his colleagues in the ballroom of the Grand Hotel. He also fell in love with the city, whose canals and imperial grandeur would remind him of St Petersburg in his years of exile. He then returned to Ustilug and thence to Clarens, where, on 17 November, suffering from a terrible toothache, he finished the sketch score of *The Rite of Spring*. The Ballets Russes were performing in Berlin, and five days later he joined them to supervise the piano rehearsal.

Stravinsky in 1913

It was during this visit to Berlin that Stravinsky had what he seems immediately to have recognised as one of the most important musical experiences of his life. On 8 December, he heard Schoenberg's song-cycle *Pierrot lunaire* conducted by the composer, whom he had met at a performance of *Petrushka* (also attended by the Kaiser) a few days earlier. He was later to describe *Pierrot lunaire* as 'the solar plexus as well as the mind of early twentieth-century music', and the work made a profound impression on him. Curiously, though, he seems not to have been tempted to explore Schoenberg's music more thoroughly; as late as 1950, he knew it hardly at all. Indeed, his relationship with Schoenberg was a notoriously troubled one. Touted by their respective admirers as leaders of two mutually exclusive schools of musical thought, for most of their careers the two men kept a wary and at times openly hostile distance. Even when they were living as near neighbours in America, they made no attempt to break the ice.

In 1912, however, the period of greatest coolness lay years ahead, and the influence of *Pierrot*'s extraordinary sound-world can perhaps be heard in the second of the *Three Japanese Lyrics*, which Stravinsky was composing at this time. These exquisite miniatures, which celebrate the coming of a spring softer than that of *The Rite*, exist in versions both for soprano and piano and for soprano and chamber orchestra. Inspired by Japanese verse and prints, Stravinsky described the pieces, not very illuminatingly, as attempts to find in music solutions analogous to those found by Japanese woodblock artists to the problems of perspective and space. Each of the songs is dedicated to a different French composer: the first to Maurice Delage and the second to Florent Schmitt. The third song is dedicated to Ravel, who heard the *Lyrics* while staying at Clarens in the spring of 1913 and whose *Trois poèmes de Stéphane Mallarmé* (Stravinsky's favourite among his friend's works) were written in their afterglow. It was during this time, too, that Stravinsky and Ravel collaborated on orchestrating the unfinished parts of Mussorgsky's opera *Khovanshchina*, which Diaghilev would present two days after the first performance of *The Rite* and which, supplanting Rimsky's version as it did, drove a final nail into the coffin of Stravinsky's relationship with his former teacher's family.

The première of *The Rite of Spring* has acquired almost mythical status in the history of twentieth-century music. It took place on 29 May 1913 at the Théâtre des Champs-Elysées in Paris and provoked a reaction beyond what any of the participants could have expected. From the moment the music began, there were sounds of protest from the auditorium. Then, when the curtain rose on Nijinsky's choreography for the 'Dances of the Adolescents' – 'a group of knock-kneed and long-braided Lolitas jumping up and down', as Stravinsky described it – uproar broke out. There were cries of outrage from the protestors, which were answered in kind by the ballet's supporters. Insults were exchanged, then blows. One man recalled his head being repeatedly pummelled by the person in the seat behind him. Aristocratic ladies shouted abuse at the performers. People even challenged one another to duels. Not a note of the music could be heard. Stravinsky himself left the hall in fury and spent the rest of the performance backstage, where he found Diaghilev flicking the house lights on and off in an attempt to restore order and Nijinsky standing on a chair shouting numbers to the dancers to keep them on cue. After the performance, however, far from weeping and reciting Pushkin in the Bois de Boulogne as legend used to have it, Stravinsky, Diaghilev and Nijinsky withdrew to a restaurant, in a mood of excitement, anger, disgust and exhilaration. Ever the showman, Diaghilev merely remarked 'Exactly what I wanted' (though his apparent equanimity is belied by the fact that he tried to make cuts in later performances, prompting one of the first of Stravinsky's many quarrels with him).

Maurice Ravel (right, with Nijinsky) around the time of his collaboration with Stravinsky on Mussorgsky's *Khovanshchina*

More than 80 years have elapsed since that first performance, and *The Rite of Spring* has established itself as one of the classics of the repertoire. It has even been used as the soundtrack to a Disney film, accompanying fanciful images of the rise and demise of the dinosaurs in *Fantasia*. But there can be few works for which familiarity has done so little to cushion the shock of the new. Its sheer musical ferocity, conveyed above all in its barbaric rhythmic drive, remains as explosive as ever. The unresolved dissonance and asymmetrical rhythms of such numbers as 'Auguries of Spring', 'Glorification of the Chosen One' and the concluding 'Sacrificial Dance' are virtually

'A group of knock-kneed and long-braided Lolitas jumping up and down': two scenes from the first production of *The Rite of Spring*, including (bottom) the notorious 'Dances of the Adolescents'

'I am the vessel through which *Le Sacre* passed': one of Stranvinsky's working drafts for *The Rite of Spring*

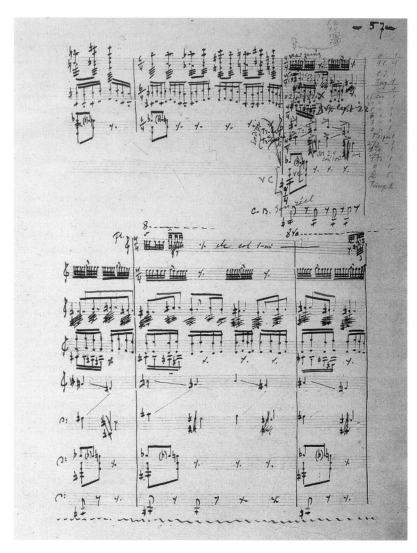

without precedent in post-Renaissance musical tradition. As the eminent Stravinsky scholar Stephen Walsh has pointed out, the composer's own sketches betray the excitement of discovery in their very calligraphy. 'I was guided by no system whatever in *Le Sacre du printemps*…' Stravinsky was later to write. 'I had only my ear to help me. I heard and I wrote what I heard. I am the vessel through which *Le Sacre* passed.' Stravinsky had looked forward eagerly to the day when he could send everything connected with his background to hell. It was with *The Rite of Spring* that he did it.

Four days after the first performance, no doubt weakened by the stress of the preceding months (during which time, in addition to his work on *The Rite*, he was involved in protracted litigation to recover a debt), the composer collapsed after eating oysters at a Paris restaurant. Typhus was diagnosed, and he was sent to a nursing home, the Villa Borghese in Neiully-sur-Seine, where he spent five weeks convalescing. His mother hurried from St Petersburg to be with him – another indication that Stravinsky's account of her may be somewhat one-sided – and he received visits from, among others, Puccini, Ravel, de Falla and Florent Schmitt. Diaghilev came too, never entering the invalid's room for fear of contagion but no doubt bringing news of *The Rite*'s reception at later performances, none of which recreated the scandal of the first. The newspapers continued to have a field day, but the music itself was beginning to gain ground with the public. On 11 July, *The Rite of Spring* was heard for the first time in London, at the Theatre Royal, Drury Lane, and went on to a run of seven performances; Monteux reported half a dozen curtain calls at one of them.

The greatest triumph, though, would come a year later, on 5 April 1914, when the first concert performance of *The Rite* in Paris was greeted ecstatically by audience and critics alike. At the end of the performance, the audience chanted Stravinsky's name in exultation and the applause seemed as if it was never going to stop. When the composer appeared, he was hoisted onto the shoulders of the crowd, who surged out of the theatre with him and carried him in triumph though the Place de la Trinité. 'The reparation is complete,' wrote one reviewer. 'Paris is rehabilitated.'

Few composers have travelled so great a distance in so little time as had Stravinsky since *The Firebird* was completed in 1910. *The Rite of Spring* had transformed not only his own musical language, but that of the century, enlarging, in Debussy's prescient words, 'the boundaries of the permissible in the empire of sound'. How he would follow it was now an urgent question both for the musical public and for Stravinsky himself. He seems already to have conceived a plan for a major new work based on Russian wedding rituals – the project which would occupy him for longer than any other single composition, finding its final form in *The Wedding* only in 1923. *The Rite*'s two immediate successors, however, were both dictated by circumstances, and both looked as much to the past as to the future.

Back in Ustilug, and still shaky after his convalescence, Stravinsky amused himself by composing the *Three Little Songs* for soprano and piano, also known as 'Recollections of my Childhood'. The first of a number of settings of Russian popular texts which he was to produce over the coming years, the *Three Little Songs* essentially belong to the period of his apprenticeship. He had played an earlier version to Rimsky-Korsakov as long ago as 1906 and had already used the theme of the last song – 'Tchitcher-Iatcher' ('The Magpie') – in the finale of the *Symphony in E Flat*.

His next large-scale work, too, predates *The Firebird* in origin. Ever since 1909, when work on it was interrupted by Diaghilev's commission for *The Firebird*, he had had on his desk the first act of an unfinished opera, *The Nightingale*, based on the fairy story by Hans Christian Andersen. He had considered reviving the opera in 1911, only to shelve it once more as he plunged into work on *The Rite of Spring*. In February 1913, however, the work was kick-started again when he was approached by the newly formed Moscow Free Theatre with a request for a three-act opera. Stravinsky initially tried to place *The Nightingale* with them in its torso form, but a month later concluded a deal to complete it in return for the irresistible sum of 10,000 roubles.

Given the pace of his musical development – working on *The Rite* in 1912, he said he felt as if 20 years, not two, had elapsed since *The Firebird* – it was a difficult task to return to a work begun under the tutelage of Rimsky-Korsakov. Stravinsky set about revising Act One, but there remains a stylistic gulf between it and Acts Two and Three, which cannot be disguised by such cosmetic links as the haunting 'Fisherman's Song', which recurs in all three. The impressionistic 'Introduction', which presents a nocturnal scene on the edge of a forest by the sea shore, could almost be by Debussy; and even in the new acts, composed during 1913 and 1914, there is a curious disharmony between, for example, the faint echoes of *The Rite* in the 'Solemn Procession' of Act Three and the conventional *chinoiserie* of the 'Chinese March' in Act Two.

For all its disparate elements, though, *The Nightingale* has a magical freshness which binds it together against the odds. Apparently a succession of tableaux, its dramatic movement is in fact strikingly faithful to that of Andersen's original. Stravinsky even preserves the skilful untheatricality of Andersen's throwaway ending, where the Emperor surprises his courtiers, who think him dead, by greeting them in full regalia. After the broad comedy of Act One, in which a gaggle of courtiers search for and finally locate the nightingale in the forest, Act Two opens in the Emperor's opulent court, where gauze curtains flutter in the breeze and a chorus of courtiers anticipates the sonorities of *The Wedding*. The curtains rise on the procession of the Emperor and his retinue, and all are charmed by the nightingale's song. Three envoys from the court of Japan then present the Emperor with a mechanical nightingale, during whose performance the real nightingale flies away and is formally banished by the Emperor. At the beginning of the third act, the Emperor is dying, surrounded by spectres of his past deeds. He calls for music and the nightingale returns, charming Death into relinquishing his prey and once more bringing tears to the Emperor's eyes. A solemn procession of courtiers arrives, expecting to find the Emperor dead, and prostrate themselves before his cheerful welcome. *The Nightingale* may not have been the work with which Stravinsky would have chosen to follow *The Rite of Spring*, but this luminous fable of the life-giving power of music clearly retained its resonance for him five years after he first conceived it.

In the event, the Moscow Free Theatre project collapsed before *The Nightingale* was finished. Instead, the work received its first performance by Diaghilev's company at the Paris Opera House on 26 May 1914, Benois' luxurious sets and costumes making it in Stravinsky's view the most beautifully staged of all his early Diaghilev works. Critics expecting another *Rite of Spring* were wrong-footed, as would happen so often during Stravinsky's career, but the music found many admirers, including Ravel and Bartók, who both claimed to detect in it the influence of Schoenberg. However, *The Nightingale*'s combination of large forces and short duration – it lasts only about 45 minutes – militated against frequent performance, and in 1916 Diaghilev asked Stravinsky to make a ballet from the opera score. The composer had already been thinking of producing a 'symphonic poem' based on the music of Acts Two and Three, and the result was *The Song of the Nightingale* (*Le Chant du rossignol*). This is the form in which the work is most often heard today, and it is an interesting reflection on the perceived inoffensiveness of the music when compared to *The Rite of Spring* that it provoked violent reactions in Switzerland, where *The Rite* had not yet been performed, as late as December 1919.

On 18 June, 10 days before the Archduke Franz Ferdinand was assassinated in Sarajevo, Stravinsky attended the London première of *The Nightingale*, where Osbert Sitwell described him taking his curtain call: 'Slight of frame, pale, about thirty years of age, with an air both worldly and abstracted, and a little angry, he bowed with solemnity to an audience that little comprehended the nature of the great musician to whom they were doing an honour.' One Sunday morning during the same visit, Stravinsky was captivated by the sound of the bells of St Paul's Cathedral and other London churches sounding

One of Benois' designs for *The Nightingale*, which Stravinsky thought the most beautifully staged of all his early Diaghilev works

together and stopped the taxi he was riding in to note down the cross-rhythms they created. The revelation of these new sonorities was a further impetus to the great project Stravinsky had been planning for at least the last two years and would work on for most of the next nine: the ballet cantata *The Wedding* (*Les Noces*). Another creative stimulus during the London trip was a performance by the clown Little Tich, whose eccentric movements are reflected in the second of the prophetic *Three Pieces for String Quartet*, which was written shortly afterwards.

In the meantime, there had been major changes in the Stravinskys' domestic life. In January 1914, Catherine had entered a sanatorium in Leysin suffering from tuberculosis, and it was here that the Stravinskys' fourth child, a daughter, Maria Milena (Milène), was born. The family moved to Leysin from Clarens the same month and installed themselves in the Grand Hotel, where Stravinsky completed *The Nightingale* at the end of March and began the *Three Pieces for String Quartet*. In the summer, they decamped again, this time to a mountain chalet near Salvan in the Valois du Rhône, before moving back to Clarens in August to rent from a new friend of Stravinsky's, the conductor Ernest Ansermet, a house next door to Les Tilleuls, where he had written *The Rite of Spring*.

Stravinsky's creative life, too, was branching out in new directions after the self-imposed detour of *The Nightingale*. The *Three Pieces for String Quartet* are, within their highly compressed compass, as ground-breaking as anything in *The Rite*, and Stravinsky thought the third of them, which directly anticipates the chorale-like endings of such works as the *Symphonies of Wind Instruments* and the late *Requiem Canticles*, among the best things

64

he had written up to that time. He was later to orchestrate the pieces as three of the *Four Studies* for orchestra under the titles 'Dance', 'Eccentric' and 'Canticle'.

During the rest of the summer, he also worked on *Pribaoutki*, a set of four songs for medium voice and eight instruments. Like 'Recollections of my Childhood', *Pribaoutki* attest to Stravinsky's fascination with popular Russian forms during the long period of gestation of *The Wedding*, serious work on which also began at around this time. The *pribaoutka* is a form of Russian popular verse, apparently developed from a type of game in which the participants make up a poem by adding words in turn at extreme speed. The four tiny songs – 'Kornilo', 'Natashka', 'The Colonel' and 'The Old Man and the Hare' – are settings of nonsense poems, in which ducks play bagpipes and old men cook soup without fire; the third poem, for example, consists almost entirely of words beginning with the letter 'p'. But the vitality and craftsmanship of these miniatures is out of all proportion to the slightness of the material. They clearly point the way ahead to the next phase of Stravinsky's so-called 'Russian period', which was to reach its apotheosis in *The Wedding*. In particular, they appear to be his first musical response to another revelation dating from this time: 'One important characteristic of Russian popular verse,' Stravinsky wrote in *Expositions and Developments*, 'is that the accents of the spoken verse are ignored when the verse is sung. The recognition of the musical possibilities inherent in this fact was one of the most rejoicing discoveries of my life'.

There was little other cause for rejoicing that summer. At the beginning of July, only days before Austria-Hungary declared war on Serbia, Stravinsky had paid a flying visit to Ustilug and Kiev to pick up some collections of Russian folk stories and poetry. On 30 July, Russia mobilised her army in support of Serbia. Two days later Germany declared war on Russia and by 4 August the conflict had drawn in all the major European powers. It would be almost half a century before Stravinsky saw the country of his birth again.

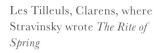

Les Tilleuls, Clarens, where Stravinsky wrote *The Rite of Spring*

Chapter 4

The loss of Russia (1914-1920)

'The greatest crisis in my life as a composer,' Stravinsky wrote in *Themes and Conclusions*, 'was the loss of Russia, and its language not only of music but of words.' In an earlier version of the same passage, he spoke of how that loss affected every circumstance of his personal as well as his artistic life and led to a decade of 'samplings, experiments, amalgamations', before he could find a clear path forward.

For some years, of course, Stravinsky had been living a cosmopolitan life, shuttling between Russia and the centres of European cultural and social activity. Since May 1910, when the family left their St Petersburg flat on the English Prospect, he had lived mainly in Switzerland, typically returning to Ustilug only for the summer months. There was no need for him to return to Russia on the outbreak of war – he had been exempted from military service on health grounds – but he could presumably have done so had he wished (and as his mother did, albeit with difficulty and the financial help of the 35-year-old Thomas Beecham). In fact, as we have seen, he moved back to Clarens, renting a cottage, La Pervenche, from Ernset Ansermet. If this was exile of a kind, it was a chosen exile. Only as the war dragged on, and especially after the cataclysm of the November Revolution of 1917, did it turn inexorably into an enforced one.

In August 1914, then, such homesickness as may have been mixed with Stravinsky's pleasure in the folk tales he had salvaged from Ustilug and Kiev was as much for the Russia of the past as for that of the present. At La Pervenche, he began to immerse himself in the nonsense rhymes of the collection *Koz'ma Prutkov*, some of which he had already set in his student days, and was only deflected from basing a large-scale work on them when Benois poured cold water on the project. He was also revisiting Afanassyev's classic collections of Russian fairy tales and legends and was starting to quarry from an anthology of wedding songs recently published by P I Kireyevsky the libretto of what was to become *The Wedding*.

It is a peculiarity of this period of Stravinsky's creative life that its central work, *The Wedding*, the composition of which spans the war years and beyond, and which is the true successor in his oeuvre to *The Rite of Spring*, does not emerge in its final form until 1923. Throughout the nine years from 1914, when work on it began in earnest, it hovers in the background, an unseen unifying presence, underpinning, shaping and being shaped by the apparently disparate compositions which surface in the foreground. In September, after a trip to Florence to discuss (and resist) a proposal from Diaghilev to create a ballet based on the mass, Stravinsky finished the fourth of the *Pribaoutki* songs. From then until August 1916, when he completed the score of his 'burlesque' *Renard*, the only compositions to escape from the gravitational field of *The Wedding* were a series of Russian songs and small-scale piano pieces.

The songs draw on the same corpus of Russian folk and popular material he turned to for *The Wedding*, and fall into five groups, including *Pribaoutki*: the *Cat's Cradle Songs*, the *Four Russian Peasant Songs*, the *Three Tales for Children*, and the *Four Russian Songs*. The four tiny *Cat's Cradle Songs* (*Berceuses du chat*) were completed in November 1915. Set for contralto and a marvellously feline ensemble of three clarinets, they are even more concentrated than the *Pribaoutki* – the longest of them lasts little more than a minute – but as with *Pribaoutki* their power far outstrips their scale. On hearing them at their first performance in June 1919, that most economical of composers Anton Webern wrote rapturously to Alban Berg of the 'indescribably touching' nature of these lullabies, the music of which moved him 'wholly and beyond belief'. Robert Craft has pointed out that sketches for the opening phrase of the cycle appear on the same sheet as those for the similar opening phrase of *The Wedding*.

In their fascination with ritual and superstition, the *Four Russian Peasant Songs* are also clearly related to *The Wedding*. Two of the four were written in December/January of 1914/15 and two in December/January of 1916/17. Scored for unaccompanied female chorus – Stravinsky added an accompaniment of four horns in 1954 – these pieces have the subtitle 'Podblyudnye', which the composer loosely translated as 'Saucers'. This refers to a kind of peasant fortune-telling in which personal items were placed in a dish of water and removed to ritual singing, including the refrain 'Slava!' or 'Glory!' which punctuates the third and fourth of the songs.

Another set of songs based on Russian folk poetry is the *Three Tales for Children* for voice and piano, which were begun in 1916 and finished in the summer of the following year. Two of the songs, 'Tilim-bom' and 'Geese and swans', were later rescored for mezzo-soprano, flute, harp and guitar as part of the *Four Songs* of 1953-54. (Confusingly, the other two songs in this later collection were rescored from yet another set, the last from these years of *The Wedding*, the *Four Russian Songs* written around the turn of the year 1918/19.)

In parallel with these flowerings of his love for Russian folk material, Stravinsky was also producing a series of piano pieces which point in other directions equally important to his future development. On 15 November 1914, he completed a little 'Polka' for piano duet, which was to form one of the *Three Easy Pieces*. It is dedicated to Diaghilev, whom it supposedly caricatures as 'a circus ring-master in evening dress and top hat, cracking his whip and urging on a rider', and to whom he played it in Italy the following year. Modest though the piece is, Stravinsky himself saw in its ironic subversion of a received genre the seeds of his later 'neo-classical' works. In December 1914, he wrote a companion piece, a 'March' dedicated to his friend and champion the Italian composer Alfredo Casella, and three months later completed the set with a rather wistful 'ice cream wagon Waltz', dedicated to Erik Satie.

Two of the dedicatees of *Three Easy Pieces*: Alfredo Casella (top) and Erik Satie. The third piece was dedicated to Diaghilev

In the early months of 1917, Stravinsky composed another set of miniatures for piano duet, the *Five Easy Pieces*. These were written for his children and are the mirror image of the earlier set in having an easy right hand and a difficult left hand part. Once again, as titles such as 'Español', 'Napoletana' and 'Galop' hint, their characteristic stance is ironic semi-detachment from the stereotypes they exploit. Stravinsky's own favourite was the third piece, 'Balalaika', which in its rotating repetition of small melodic cells over an ostinato bass belongs perhaps more obviously than its companions to a line of development from *The Rite* through the first of the *Three Pieces for String Quartet* to *The Wedding*. All eight of the piano duet pieces were later orchestrated and regrouped to form the two *Suites* for small orchestra.

Samplings, experiments, amalgamations – but behind them lay near-continuous work on *The Wedding*. The ballet was seldom out of Stravinsky's thoughts. In January 1915, the family moved to the Hôtel Victoria at Château d'Oex, where the mountain air was thought to be better for Catherine's deteriorating health, and during a quick visit to Clarens to tidy up some administrative loose ends Stravinsky jotted down in his railway carriage the hiccuping song of a couple of drunks, which was later incorporated into *The Wedding*'s final scene. The following month, in Rome to hear the first Italian concert performance of *Petrushka*, he took the opportunity to play what he had so far written of the work to Diaghilev. The great impresario was moved to tears by what he heard, a reaction which led Stravinsky to dedicate the work to him. During the same visit, Stravinsky met Gerald Tyrwhitt, later Lord Berners and a staunch advocate of his music, and the 24-year-old Sergey Prokofiev, whom Diaghilev had recently commissioned to produce a ballet on a Russian prehistoric theme. (The result of this commission, *Ala and Lolly*, failed to satisfy Diaghilev, but the music was recycled as *The Scythian Suite*, a work whose transparent debt to *The Rite of Spring* is one of the clearest reminders of Stravinsky's influence on his younger contemporaries during these years.)

Ever since August 1914, the future had looked very bleak for the Ballets Russes. The outbreak of hostilities had put paid to Diaghilev's plans to take the company to Berlin in the autumn, and it soon became clear that the exigencies of war would make it impossible for him to operate in Europe on the old footing. Never a man to be daunted by obstacles, however, Diaghilev immediately redirected his sights to the New World and began stitching together plans to take the Ballets Russes to New York. In March 1915, he too moved his base of operations to neutral Switzerland, renting the Villa Bellerive at Ouchy with the current nucleus of his troupe, which included Léon Bakst, the artists Mikhail Larionov and Natalya Goncharova, and

Members of Diaghilev's 'colony' at Ouchy in 1915: (from left to right) Léonide Massine, Natalya Goncharova, Mikhail Larionov, Stravinsky, Léon Bakst

Diaghilev's new choreographic wunderkind, the 19-year-old Léonide Massine. (A notable absentee was Vaslav Nijinsky, whose marriage to a Hungarian dance student in 1913 had provoked a dramatic break with Diaghilev; he was currently interned in Hungary as an enemy alien.) Stravinsky soon moved to nearby Morges, the lakeside town which was to be his home until 1920, and was able to cycle over on a regular basis; he later described this period as his 'bicycle phase'. Diaghilev remained as outwardly confident as ever, loftily referring to Ouchy as his 'colony'. Not until the last days of 1915, however, would the company mount another performance.

Stravinsky's fortunes had been intertwined with Diaghilev's for the last five years, and this downturn affected him directly. The Ballets Russes had been his main source of commissions, and with nothing coming in from Diaghilev he was forced to look elsewhere. The situation was made even worse by the fact that the European office of his publishers was based in enemy territory in Berlin, and that, with all communications strained by the war, income from his estate in Ustilug could no longer be relied upon. Help was not long in coming, however. For some years his friend the Singer sewing machine heiress Princess Edmond de Polignac had been discussing possible new commissions with him. In December 1915, the composer made his conducting debut with *The Firebird* in a pair of concerts given by Diaghilev's company before they set sail for New York. The second of these took place in Paris, where, after Diaghilev's departure, Stravinsky visited the Princess and received a formal commission, and a welcome fee of 2,500 Swiss francs, for the composition he had already been working on for some months.

This was the burlesque *Renard*. A farmyard fable drawn from Afanassyev, it tells the story of a fox who tries to lure a self-important cock down from his perch by subterfuge. Twice he succeeds and twice the cock jumps – a moment known as the *salto mortale* and preceded by a circus-ring drumroll – only to be saved from death on both occasions by the intervention of a cat and a goat, who finally strangle the offending fox. Stravinsky's treatment of this folktale is highly individual. The work is scored for two tenors and two basses, and an unusual chamber ensemble of percussion, timpani, cimbalom and string quintet. The setting places the story at a number of removes from reality. For one thing, the entire action is effectively presented twice in succession. For another, the singers are deliberately not identified with the animal protagonists – the characters' actions are performed by clowns or dancing acrobats, and there is no consistency as to which or how many singers present

'That curious American woman who looked like Dante and whose ambition it was to have her bust next to Richelieu's in the Louvre': the Princess Edmond de Polignac

their words. Furthermore, the players enter and leave at the beginning and end of the piece to the strains of a little march, the rambunctious gusto of which sets the tone for the whole spectacle. In case this is not enough to remind us that it's only a performance, Stravinsky's libretto ends with the singers asking the audience for a donation!

The dominant sonority of *Renard* is provided by the cimbalom, a multi-stringed dulcimer which is struck with spoon-shaped wooden sticks. Stravinsky had discovered this instrument one evening in January 1915 when Ansermet had introduced him to the Hungarian cimbalomist Aladar Racz at Maxim's restaurant in Geneva. Fascinated by its possibilities, he conscripted Racz to help him buy one – apparently from an old Hungarian gypsy – and taught himself to play it. For a while he even composed at it, forsaking his usual practice of working at the piano. (The instrument also defines the texture of the 1918 *Ragtime* and early drafts of *The Wedding*, and at one point Stravinsky actually commissioned the Pleyel company to make him a mechanical version equivalent to the pianola.) In *Renard*, the cimbalom introduces each appearance of the fox with a flourish reminiscent of the piano arpeggios which announce the eponymous songbird in *The Nightingale*; it also makes shift for the gusli, an extinct Russian balalaika, in the 'nice little song' the cat and the goat sing towards the end of the piece. But its unique timbre, at once exotic and honky-tonk, permeates the whole work, contributing to what Stephen Walsh has perfectly described as its 'village-band flavour'. *Renard* was completed in August 1916, but in what must be counted a major lost opportunity for raising wartime spirits, was not performed until 1922.

It is to the Princess Edmond de Polignac too that we owe a fascinating glimpse of the Stravinskys' domestic life during the time *Renard* was being written. One evening in 1916, the composer asked her to dinner at the second of their Morges addresses, the Villa Rogie Vue, and met her at Lausanne for the last half-hour of the train journey. 'Everything was covered with snow,' she wrote,

'and it was a quiet, clear, moonlight night, very still, and not very cold. I shall always remember the happy impression I had as Stravinsky took me into his house, for it looked to me like a Christmas tree, brilliantly lighted up and decorated in the warm colours that the Russian Ballet had brought to Paris.

'Madame Stravinsky was a striking figure: pale, thin, full of dignity and grace, she at once gave me the impression of nobility of race and grace that was confirmed by all she did in the following years. In the warmth of her charming house she looked like a princess in a Russian fairy tale: surrounded by her delicate children...'

She went on to describe a luxuriant Russian supper of numerous courses served at a table brilliantly illuminated with coloured candles and bedecked with fruit and flowers, a meal she would remember for the rest of her life. Perhaps with the benefit of hindsight, though, she also sensed an undertow of tragedy to the entire evening.

In May, while Stravinsky was still hard at work on *Renard*, he received a telegram from Diaghilev inviting him to join the ballet company in Madrid. Despite wartime travel restrictions, he arrived in Spain within days and stayed for a month. The visit, his first, left him enthralled with the country. He attended a couple of bullfights, went sightseeing in Toledo and at the Escorial, acknowledged the applause of ecstatic audiences for *The Firebird* and *Petrushka*, and generally revelled in his celebrity status. He was entertained by the royal family, and established a lasting friendship with the Spanish composer Manuel de Falla, whom he described as the shyest man he had ever met. He may also have had a romance with the ballerina who danced the role of *The Firebird* at the Teatro Real, Lydia Lopokova (the future wife of John Maynard Keynes). The music of the streets and taverns captivated him too, surfacing the following year in his *Study for Pianola* (retitled 'Madrid' in its later orchestrated version) and in the *pasodoble* 'Royal March' from *The Soldier's Tale* of 1918.

The shyest man Stravinsky had ever met: the Spanish composer Manuel de Falla (1876-1946)

The Spanish trip seems to have restored damaged relations with Diaghilev, whose failure to include Stravinsky in his American retinue had rankled with the composer. The impresario greeted him on his arrival in Madrid with the words 'I have been waiting for you like a brother', and in September they were together again in San Sebastian, from where Stravinsky accompanied Diaghilev to Bordeaux to see him off to his second New York season.

1917 was a momentous year in the history of the century. For Stravinsky it began inauspiciously enough with convalescence after another attack of intercostal neuralgia, which temporarily paralysed his legs. Then in March came the news of the Liberal Revolution in Russia (generally known as the February Revolution because of the difference in calendars). Stravinsky's excitement at these heady events recalls Wordsworth's reaction to the French Revolution. To his mother and Yury he wrote: 'All my thoughts are with you in these unforgettable days of happiness that are sweeping across our dear, liberated Russia'. He even made plans for returning to his homeland, though in the event these came to nothing. Instead, the family moved to their third and final Morges residence in May – a second-floor flat in the seventeenth-century Maison Bornand, where the pianist, composer and future Polish premier Paderewski was one of their neighbours.

In Rome in April, Stravinsky conducted *The Firebird* and *Fireworks* at a concert organised by Diaghilev in support of the Italian Red Cross. Normally, such a performance would have been preceded by a rendition of the Russian Imperial Anthem 'God Save the Tsar', but since Nicholas II had just abdicated in favour of a Provisional Government, something else was needed, and quickly. Diaghilev hit on the traditional 'Song of the Volga Boatmen', and Stravinsky set to work to provide a performing version, dictating the instrumentation note by note to Ansermet shortly before the concert. The performance of *Fireworks* was accompanied by an innovative light-show designed by the Futurist painter, Giacomo Balla. Diaghilev later threw a big reception at the Grand Hotel, at which there was an exhibition of Futurist pictures. Stravinsky, who was something of a hero for the movement, has left an affectionate pen-portrait of the Futurists: they 'were not the aeroplanes they wanted to be', he wrote in his *Conversations*, 'but they were at any rate a pack of very nice, noisy Vespas.' If any parallel can be drawn between Stravinsky's work and a movement in the visual arts, however, it is with the fractured planes and multiple perspectives of Cubism that his music of the period has more in common.

Autoritratto by Giacomo Balla of the Futurists, whom Stravinsky described as 'a pack of very nice, noisy Vespas'

Pablo Picasso and Léonide
Massine at Pompeii in 1917
during their collaboration on
Satie's *Parade*

Erik Satie's ballet *Parade* was one of the other works
scheduled for performance by the Ballets Russes in the spring
of 1917. *Parade* was a collaboration between Satie and Cocteau
and embodied some of the ideas in which Cocteau had failed to
interest Stravinsky when discussing a proposed ballet (*David*)
with him in 1914. Most important for Stravinsky's future,
though, was the fact that *Parade* was designed by Pablo Picasso.
The great Spanish artist, between whom and Stravinsky
comparisons were already being made in 1917, was in Rome
working on the sets at the same time Stravinsky was there, and
it is from these weeks that their friendship dates.

A map of fortifications?
Picasso's first portrait of
Stravinsky, 1917

Iṣor STRAWINSKY

Almost the same age, both protean self-reinventors perpetually open to new experiences and influences, the two men now seen as arguably the pre-eminent figures of the century in their respective arts seem to have hit it off straight away. Picasso made the first of his three drawings of Stravinsky and decorated the manuscript of the 'Song of the Volga Boatmen' with a red circle as a symbol of the Revolution. They toured the sights of Naples together, spending hours at the aquarium and combing the backstreet dealers' shops for Neapolitan watercolours. They even contrived to get arrested together one night for urinating against a wall of the Galleria; Stravinsky insisted on being taken across the road to the San

76

Carlo Opera, where the policeman let them go after hearing them addressed as 'maestri'. (Picasso seems to have had a knack of getting Stravinsky into trouble, even when he wasn't present: as the composer made his way back to Morges in April he was detained at the border when the military authorities found Picasso's full-face drawing of him in his luggage and took it for a secret plan of fortifications. This time only an appeal to Lord Berners at the British Embassy ensured a happy outcome!) Perhaps the most prescient encounter for both artists' future careers was a visit they paid to the *commedia dell'arte* together. The performance took place in a crowded little room reeking of garlic, and, as Stravinsky recalled in his *Conversations*, 'the Pulcinella was a great drunken lout whose every gesture, and probably every word if I had understood it, was obscene.' Two years later, his ballet *Pulcinella* was the subject of one of his most successful collaborations. The designer was Pablo Picasso.

Shortly after he got back to Morges, Stravinsky was returning from a lunch in Lausanne when he found a man in mourning clothes in his garden. When the composer asked him what he was doing there, the stranger replied: 'It appears that there has been a death in the house'. Bertha, Stravinsky's old nurse, who had joined the family in Switzerland at the beginning of the war, had died of a ruptured blood-vessel. Stravinsky was prostrated with grief and unable to work for weeks, retiring to the mountains to spend the summer in a chalet near Diablerets. (Here he met André Gide to discuss the possibility of composing the incidental music for a production of Shakespeare's *Antony and Cleopatra* in the French novelist's translation, but the projected collaboration came to nothing. The idea of working together remained in both their minds, however, and in the 1930s they finally collaborated, albeit none too happily, on Stravinsky's ballet *Persephone*.) The composer had barely resumed his oft-interrupted work on *The Wedding* in August when he received the news of a second death – that of his favourite brother Gury, who had succumbed to typhus at Iasi on the Romanian Front, where he had been serving in a Red Cross unit. Although the brothers had met infrequently in recent years, they had retained a place in each other's affections, and the news instilled in Stravinsky a deep sense of loneliness. Despite his grief, however, he was finally able to complete an orchestral draft of *The Wedding* on 11 October.

No other single work of Stravinsky's occupied him for so long or went through so many changes of instrumentation as *The Wedding*. The work had been conceived during the composition of *The Rite of Spring* and the voices were originally to have been accompanied by a mammoth orchestra, with prominent parts for guitars and gusli. The orchestra is greatly reduced in the 1917 version, which includes parts for cimbalom, piano and harpsichord, and for which Stravinsky envisaged the different instrumental groups physically separated from one another on the stage. In 1919, he conceived a version for two cimbaloms, mechanical piano, harmonium and percussion, but eventually abandoned this and various later attempts to combine pianolas and played instruments because of coordination difficulties. Only in 1922 did he suddenly hit on the final ensemble of four pianos and percussion, in which form the work received its first performance, by Diaghilev's company, in 1923.

The Wedding: Felia Doubrovska as the bride in the 1923 première

The Wedding is one of Stravinsky's greatest achievements and ranks among the masterpieces of twentieth-century music. The composer described it as 'a suite of typical wedding episodes told through quotations of typical talk', and the work's seamless elision of ritual and ribaldry gives it a compendious breadth, the impact of which is at once intensely human and intensely spiritual. As in *Renard*, the voices are not identified with the protagonists, but here the effect is less to distance the action than to universalise it. At the same time, with its loving recreation of peasant customs and its deep roots in liturgical chant, *The Wedding* is Stravinsky's most uncompromisingly Russian work. The composer described the ensemble of pianos and percussion as 'perfectly homogeneous, perfectly impersonal, and perfectly mechanical'; in performance, however, the impression is rather of immense clarity, brightness and dynamic force. The work's motoric drive is felt even in its least headlong episodes. Nowhere is Stravinsky's dictum that 'pulsation is the reality of music' more clearly embodied: as his friend and collaborator of these years C F Ramuz remarked, *The Wedding* 'is swept from end to end with a single current'.

In the first of the work's four scenes the bride laments the loss of her virginity as the bridesmaids braid her hair; the second takes place in the bridegroom's house; the third presents the bride's departure and ends with a moving lament for the two mothers. The fourth and final scene is a wedding feast, complete with the aforementioned hiccuping drunks and preparation of the marital bed. The libretto concludes with a solemn invocation by the bridegroom to 'let us live in happiness so that all men may envy us', and *The Wedding* closes with its only extended instrumental passage, in which the chiming of bell and pianos resonates in the intervening silences in a coda of profound and timeless mystery.

A month after the first orchestral score of *The Wedding* was completed, the November Revolution brought the Bolsheviks to power in Russia. This was altogether a different proposition from the Liberal Revolution Stravinsky had greeted with such excitement earlier in the year, and his enthusiasm for the new order quickly evaporated. So too did the revenues from his estate in Ustilug and, as Russia descended into civil war in the wake of the Treaty of Brest-Litovsk, any remaining prospect of repatriation.

For the first time in his life, Stravinsky found himself in real financial difficulties. He had a sick wife and four children to support in a foreign country in the midst of a Europe

Exile confirmed:
the storming of the Winter
Palace, St Petersburg,
November 1917

immobilised by war. Not only was he now without the unearned income from Ustilug which had always underpinned his finances; Diaghilev's company was still struggling to keep going and could no longer be relied upon for commissions or royalties. These straitened circumstances, shared to a greater or lesser extent by many of the artists who formed the circle of his acquaintance in Switzerland, were the spur to the creation of one of Stravinsky's most original works, *The Soldier's Tale* (*L'Histoire du soldat*). The idea was to produce a piece of music theatre which required very little staging and could therefore be toured to village halls as well as to more conventional venues. The work would be spoken, played and danced, but the music could also be performed separately. The concept had occurred to Stravinsky in the spring of 1917, but composition began in earnest only in 1918. His principal collaborator on the project was his friend the novelist C F Ramuz, a kind and lively man with whom he had worked on the French translations of *Renard* and *The Wedding* and whose reminiscences of the composer, published in 1929, have fascinated Stravinsky scholars as much as they offended their subject. The two men, together with Ansermet and the Swiss painter René Auberjonois, who was to design the piece, set about finding patronage for the new work. After many approaches to potential backers, they finally co-opted the support of Werner Reinhart, a wealthy Swiss patron and amateur clarinettist, who was rewarded for his sponsorship with the dedication of *The Tale* and a set of *Three Pieces for Clarinet Solo*. (Ramuz' own reward came some 20 years later, in the form of a little musical tribute for his sixtieth birthday – the *Petit Ramusianum harmonique*.)

Stravinsky and Ramuz extracted the narrative of *The Soldier's Tale* from a number of Afanassyev's stories about a soldier's encounters with the devil. In their version, a soldier returning to his village on a fortnight's leave is met by the devil in disguise, who swaps a magic book for the soldier's violin and invites him to stay with him for three days. At the end of his stay, however, the soldier finds that not three days but three years have passed and that he is permanently alienated from his home. This is the starting point for a series of encounters with the devil in various guises, during the course of which the soldier meets and marries a princess and achieves some outward success in life. He remains dissatisfied, however, and at the end of *The Tale* tries to return to his native village, only to lose both the princess and his soul in a final encounter with the prince of darkness.

The music of *The Soldier's Tale* is scored for clarinet, bassoon, cornet à pistons, trombone, violin, double-bass and percussion – an idiosyncratic ensemble Stravinsky claimed was influenced by his recent discovery of jazz – and its texture has a rasping spareness far removed from that of *The Wedding*. There is, too, in the music of the 'Pastorale', when the soldier realises how long he has been away from home, a new note of desolation which, for all his denial of an autobiographical element in his work, it is hard not to connect with Stravinsky's own recognition of exile.

Russian though its origins are, *The Soldier's Tale* has none of the specifically Russian flavour of *The Wedding* or the songs, and Stravinsky was later to describe it as his 'final break with the Russian orchestral school'. Indeed, he and Ramuz went out of their way to stress the work's internationalism

81

and contemporaneity. The music's borrowings from a range of international popular forms are strikingly evident – ragtime and tango in the 'Three Dances', the *pasodoble* in the 'Royal March' – and at its first performance the narrator wore evening dress and the soldier a modern Swiss army private's uniform. That performance took place in the Théâtre Municipal in Lausanne on 28 September 1918 and was intended to kick off a regional tour. In the event, the series fell victim to the Spanish flu epidemic which was to engulf Europe in the months after the First World War, and it was years before *The Soldier's Tale* was staged again. Despite this early neglect, however, it remains, particularly in its concert suite form, one of Stravinsky's most popular works.

Stravinsky with his collaborator on *The Soldier's Tale*, the novelist C F Ramuz (1878-1947)

Jazz influences are also explicit in two other pieces composed during and after *The Tale*, the *Ragtime* for 11 instruments and the *Piano-Rag-Music*. Stravinsky had not yet heard jazz performed, but had seen some ragtime sheet music Ansermet brought back from the States after Diaghilev's American tour and was struck by its possibilities for expanding his own musical language. He was later tellingly to describe the two pieces as composite concert portraits of the new music, in the same way that Chopin's waltzes or mazurkas are concert portraits of their respective dance models.

Ragtime was finished in unforgettable circumstances on the morning of 11 November 1918. In *Dialogues* the composer himself wrote:

'I remember how, sitting at the cimbalom in my garret in Morges… I was aware of a buzzing in my ears that increased until I was afraid I had been stricken like Robert Schumann. I went down to the street and was told that everyone was hearing the same noise and that it was from cannon along the French frontier announcing the end of the war.'

Ragtime also exists in a piano arrangement, for the first published edition of which Picasso drew the front cover – a famous picture of two musicians created from the ramifications of a single continuous line. The *Piano-Rag-Music* was written in 1919 for the virtuoso pianist Artur Rubinstein, whom Stravinsky had met in London in 1914, but Rubinstein hated it and performed it as little as possible.

At the beginning of 1919, Stravinsky completed a new *Firebird* suite and the *Four Russian Songs*, and in the spring travelled to Paris for his first meeting with Diaghilev for more than a year. Relations between the two men seem never fully to have recovered from their falling-out over the Ballets Russes' American tour in 1915/16, and much of the following summer would be spent in a quarrel by proxy over payment of performance fees on *The Firebird* and *Petrushka* (a matter which had no doubt acquired greater urgency for Stravinsky since December 1918, when the size of his household, and the number of his dependants, had doubled with the arrival of Catherine's sister's family as refugees from Russia.) At the root of the disagreement, though, was Diaghilev's jealousy of Stravinsky's new patrons. The impresario hated his protégés to work for other masters, and was outraged that Stravinsky had written *Renard* and *The Soldier's Tale* not for him but for the Princess de Polignac and Werner Reinhart. Nonetheless, this spring meeting sowed the seeds for Stravinsky's next major composition, a work which would change the direction of his musical development in ways neither he nor Diaghilev could have imagined when the latter first broached the subject:

'The suggestion that was to lead to *Pulcinella* came from Diaghilev
one spring afternoon while we were walking together in the Place de
la Concorde: "Don't protest at what I am about to say. I know you are
much taken by your Alpine colleagues" – this was said with withering
contempt – "but I have an idea that I think will amuse you more than
anything they can propose. I want you to look at some delightful
eighteenth-century music with the idea of orchestrating it for a
ballet." When he said that the composer was Pergolesi, I thought he
must be deranged... I did promise to look, however, and to give him
my opinion.

'I looked, and I fell in love.'

What Diaghilev had in mind was a straightforward
orchestration which would cater to the current vogue for
eighteenth- and nineteenth-century pastiche. He had scored a
hit in Rome in 1917 with Massine's choreographic debut,
The Good-humoured Ladies, the music of which was arranged by

Vincenzo Tommasini from works by Domenico Scarlatti. *La Boutique fantasque*, Respighi's orchestration of pieces by Rossini, would prove equally successful in London in June 1919. *Pulcinella* was conceived as a *commedia dell'arte* stirring of the same pot, and was presented to Stravinsky with the added incentives of collaboration with Picasso and Massine.

Back in his attic study at the Maison Bornand in Morges, Stravinsky began work on *Pulcinella* in September, composing directly onto the Pergolesi manuscripts 'as if I were correcting an old work of my own'. (In fact, scholars have since shown very few of the originals actually to have been by Pergolesi himself.) He claimed to have worked without preconceptions or aesthetic attitudes and with no idea of how the piece would turn out. It certainly didn't turn out as Diaghilev had expected: 'my music so shocked him,' Stravinsky recalled, 'that he went about for a long time with a look that suggested The Offended Eighteenth Century. In fact, however, the remarkable thing about *Pulcinella* is not how much but how little has been added or changed.'

In that last statement lies the paradox of *Pulcinella*. Much ink has been spilt in an attempt to define what makes this outwardly most uncharacteristic work also so quintessentially Stravinskyan. But despite the superficial accessibility of its music, the essence of *Pulcinella* eludes analysis to a greater degree than many of Stravinsky's more obviously demanding scores. The Baroque harmonies are thickened here, spiked with modernity there. Rhythms are sprung from the foursquare regularity of the manuscripts, and the instrumentation idiomatically recoloured. Above all, they are fused into a new formal unity. But little is lost of the substance of the originals even as they become wholly Stravinsky's own. Indeed, it is almost as if Stravinsky has liberated their true character. As one critic has remarked, hearing the (putative) Pergolesi pieces on which the ballet is based is like hearing imitations of which *Pulcinella* is the original. Perhaps Stravinsky himself best expressed the nature of the synthesis when he said that in writing *Pulcinella* he had repeated Pergolesi in his own accent.

If Diaghilev was originally shocked by the use Stravinsky had made of his new commission, he was equally disconcerted by the way Picasso responded to it. His first set of designs, which were for Offenbach-period costumes, were so far from Diaghilev's original conception that he threw them on the floor and stamped on them! In the end, though, Diaghilev got his way, and proved once again his acuity in judging an audience. The first performance of *Pulcinella*, with Picasso's *commedia dell'arte* sets and costumes and Massine's choreography, took place under Ansermet in the Paris Opera House on 15 May 1920 and was a huge success. Afterwards, Prince Firouz of Persia threw a party at a nearby château, where Stravinsky, drunk on champagne and success, stripped the bedrooms of their linen and pillow-fought with the other members of the company until three o'clock in the morning.

Picasso and Stravinsky (a little the worse for drink) in a caricature by Jean Cocteau

If the Paris audience was delighted, however, Stravinsky's apparent desertion of the modernist fold in *Pulcinella* outraged many of his erstwhile supporters. It was the first and most striking of those changes of musical direction which would, over the years of his long composing career, leave many observers bewildered and offended, struggling to catch up again just when they thought they had understood him. For Stravinsky himself, however, *Pulcinella* was as important as a signpost to the future as for itself. '*Pulcinella* was my discovery of the past,' he wrote in *Expositions and Developments*, 'the epiphany through which all my late work became possible.' Both musically and in fact, it was 'the swan song of [his] Swiss years'. By the time *Pulcinella* received its London première at the Royal Opera House, Covent Garden on 10 June 1920, Stravinsky and his family had already moved to France.

Chapter 5

Art and profession (1920-1927)

With the war over, Stravinsky had originally planned to move to Rome, where he would be closer to the European cultural mainstream than he had felt in Switzerland. He conscripted the help of various friends to put out feelers for him in the Italian capital, but despite their efforts he could find no accommodation to suit him there. France therefore became his home by default. Originally a fallback choice, it was to remain his base of operations for almost two decades.

Ernest Ansermet, Diaghilev, Stravinsky and Prokofiev, about 1920

However, two major changes in the pattern of Stravinsky's life between the wars meant that for much of that time home was less of a fixed point than it had been at any stage since he left St Petersburg. The first was his meeting with Vera de Bosset Sudeikina, the woman who was to become his constant companion for the next 50 years. The second was his development from 1924 of a career as conductor and pianist – what he called his 'profession' – which ran in parallel to (and often interfered with the practice of) his 'art', and took him all over the world on tours lasting sometimes months at a stretch. The effects of these changes would be far-reaching indeed.

The Stravinsky family spent the summer at Cantarec, a fishing village in Brittany, where the composer grumbled about the rain and the holidaymakers. It was here that he worked on the immediate successors to *Pulcinella*: the *Concertino* for string quartet and the *Symphonies of Wind Instruments*. Both were finished at Garches, the home outside Paris of the fashion designer Gabrielle 'Coco' Chanel, to which the Stravinskys moved in the autumn, and where he also wrote the set of eight piano miniatures known as *The Five Fingers* (*Les Cinq doigts*).

The *Concertino* had been commissioned as early as 1919 by the Flonzaley Quartet, who had also commissioned – as so often with Stravinsky, some time after composition had begun – the 1914 *Three Pieces for String Quartet*. The *Concertino* is in a single movement with a concertante part for the first violin and a contrasting slow central section, the tempo of which returns briefly at the end. Much later (1952) the composer arranged it for 12 instruments.

Far more important in Stravinsky's oeuvre is the other composition he was working on during these months, the *Symphonies of Wind Instruments*. The origins of this extraordinary work lay in a request from the *Revue Musicale* for a musical tribute to Debussy, who had died in March 1918. Stravinsky, who had been greatly moved by his last visit to the dying composer, produced the solemn chorale which forms the final section of the *Symphonies* and which appeared separately in a piano version in the Debussy memorial issue of the *Revue* in December 1920. The rest of the work was finished at the end of November, though it was significantly rescored in 1947.

The *Symphonies* is widely regarded as one of Stravinsky's greatest achievements and has exerted a fascination over composers as various as Sir Michael Tippett, Pierre Boulez and Karlheinz Stockhausen. Far from being symphonic in the nineteenth-century sense, the work takes its title from the root meaning of 'symphonies' as 'soundings together'. In many ways the summation of Stravinsky's so-called 'Russian period', it is revolutionary in its construction from episodes juxtaposed without transition but bound together by strict tempo relationships. Its spare, chiming, chant-like timbres have affinities with *The Wedding*, and its use of folksong-like melodic cells recalls *The Rite of Spring*. But for all that its stylistic continuities with Stravinsky's other works can be demonstrated in detail, in its effect on the ear the *Symphonies* remains *sui generis*. The composer himself described it as 'an austere ritual which is unfolded in terms of short litanies between different groups of homogeneous instruments' and as 'an objective cry of wind instruments, in place of the warm human tone of the strings' (strings virtually disappear from his writing for the next six years). Austere it may be, but the *Symphonies of Wind Instruments* is certainly not lacking in humanity: indeed, it has been described as one of the finest tributes ever dedicated by one composer to the memory of another.

The *Symphonies* received its first performance in London on 10 June 1921 and was met with blank incomprehension. This was no doubt due partly to Koussevitzky's bizarre direction of the concert. Not only was the work under-rehearsed; it also followed Rimsky-Korsakov's fulsome orchestral march from *The Golden Cockerel* without any rearrangement of the platform. The small group of 21 instrumentalists was therefore stranded at the back of the Queen's Hall stage, with a no-man's-land of empty chairs and music-stands between them and the conductor. To cap it all, Koussevitzky responded to Stravinsky's understandable criticism with a newspaper review in which he slated the work he had just premièred! There may have been some consolation for Stravinsky, though, in the fact that only three days earlier, in the very same hall, he had attended the first English concert performance of *The Rite of Spring*, which was greeted with what the conductor of the night, Eugene Goossens, described as 'hysterical enthusiasm'. The London revival of the ballet was staged by the Ballets Russes to equal acclaim a couple of weeks later. (This staging was choreographed by Massine; Nijinsky's original choreography had long been lost, and Nijinsky, who had left the company in 1917, was by now enmeshed in the schizophrenia which blighted the last 30 years of his life.) The composer was lionised by the London circuit and enjoyed every minute of it.

In the meantime, there had been significant developments in Stravinsky's private life. The onset of Catherine's tuberculosis in 1914 had apparently brought to an end the sexual side of their marriage, and while they were living at Garches

Stravinsky began an affair with 'Coco' Chanel. At around the same time, he also had a brief romance with 'Katinka', a dancer at the Chauve-Souris nightclub, whose theme tune he added to his 1921 orchestration of the 'Polka' from *Three Easy Pieces*. These entanglements were surely as influential as Catherine's health in his decision to move his family out of Paris, and in May he officially relocated to Biarritz. By then, however, he had acquired a studio in the Maison Pleyel, the pianola factory which was to be his Paris home for the next 12 years (and provided him with the most eccentric of his many addresses!).

The seafront at Biarritz, to which the Stravinsky family moved in 1921

25   BIARRITZ. — Le Casino Municipal. — L'Hôtel du Palais et le Phare. — LL.

By then, too, he had met Vera Sudeikina.

Born Vera de Bosset in St Petersburg in 1888, Vera Sudeikina was 32 years old and had only recently arrived in Paris. Of French and Swedish parentage, she had been brought up on the family estate at Gorky, between St Petersburg and Moscow, like Stravinsky in the care of a German governess. She subsequently attended boarding school in Moscow, acquiring a reputation as a rebel (again like Stravinsky) before graduating to university in Berlin. She returned to Moscow in 1914 and, despite being too tall and too old to make a professional ballerina, she entered the Nelidova Ballet School to develop her stage presence. The theatre had been her first love and by now she was carving out a career on stage and screen. She had also married a compulsive gambler, whom she left in 1916 to elope to St Petersburg with the bisexual painter Serge Sudeikin, himself married and a former lover of Diaghilev. In the Russian capital they moved in the literary circles which revolved around the Stray Dog cabaret, and their friends included the poets Anna Akhmatova and Osip Mandelstam. Caught, literally as well as metaphorically, in the crossfire of the 1917 Revolution, she fled with Sudeikin to the Crimea, where the couple married without divorcing their previous partners. In 1919, as the Red Army advanced into the Crimea, they fled again, ending up in Tiflis (Tbilisi), where they lived for a year. From there they made their way to Paris in May 1920, just nine months before Vera's first meeting with Stravinsky.

That meeting took place on 19 February 1921 in an Italian restaurant in Montmartre, to which Diaghilev had invited her for dinner with friends. One of the friends was Stravinsky, whom Vera found the wittiest and most amusing man she had ever met. By the summer they were lovers – they always celebrated 14 July as their 'wedding anniversary' – and were organising their lives to ensure that they spent as much time together as possible.

While he was in London, Stravinsky had discussed two new projects with Diaghilev, and on his return to France he began to work on them in earnest, first in the beach-house at Anglet, near Bayonne, where the family spent the summer (and where he also wrote, for Artur Rubinstein, the virtuosic piano transcription *Three Pieces from Petrushka*), and subsequently in the Châlet des Rochers in the centre of Biarritz, to which they moved in October. The first of these projects was the orchestration of two numbers for Tchaikovsky's *The Sleeping Beauty*, which Diaghilev was planning to stage in London in November and which had never before been seen in Western Europe. The 'Variation d'Aurore' and the Act 2 'Entr'acte' had been cut after the first performance in St Petersburg and never reinstated in the score; Stravinsky worked from a piano reduction of the pieces. He threw himself wholeheartedly into the venture. His *Autobiography* bears witness to his love for Tchaikovsky, then a deeply unfashionable composer in progressive Western circles, as does the open letter he wrote to *The Times* in praise of the Russian master. He was also clearly impressed by Diaghilev's courage in mounting a production of a work regarded as *démodé* by precisely those elements to whom the Ballets Russes had always most appealed. Above all, as he wrote in his *Autobiography*, he felt a 'profound admiration for classical ballet, which in its very essence, by the beauty of its *ordonnance* and the aristocratic austerity of its forms, so closely corresponds with my conception of art. For here, in classical dancing, I see the triumph of studied conception over vagueness, of the rule over the arbitrary, of order over the haphazard.' This is precisely what Stravinsky was striving to achieve in the works of what, despite his own rejection of the term 'neo-classicism' as 'a much abused expression meaning absolutely nothing', is still generally called his 'neo-classical' period – a period usually taken to run from *Pulcinella* in 1920 to *The Rake's Progress* in 1951, but encompassing music of such extraordinary variety as to stretch the term to the limits of its usefulness.

The second project Stravinsky discussed with Diaghilev in London was directly inspired by the revival of *The Sleeping Beauty*, and is often seen as the curtain-raiser to that neo-classical period. This was *Mavra*, a one-act *opera buffa* based on Pushkin's verse story *The Little House in Kolomna*. Diaghilev's young personal secretary Boris Kochno was enlisted to write the libretto, which tells the story of Parasha, the daughter of a middle-class Russian family in the time of Charles X, and her love for a hussar called Basil. The entire action consists of Parasha tricking her mother into taking Basil on as a cook – Mavra – by dressing him in women's clothes, only to have the ruse exposed when the 'cook' is discovered shaving, at which point the hussar leaps out of the window and runs away. On this calculatedly trivial framework, Stravinsky hangs half an hour of music which has often been described as an aesthetic manifesto. The score is prefaced by a dedication to the memory of Pushkin, Glinka and Tchaikovsky, with whom, as against the nationalist tradition represented by 'the Five' (including Rimsky), the composer explicitly aligned himself in his published statements about the work, beginning with an open letter to *Le Figaro* around the time of the first performance. Whereas in *Renard* the action had been distanced by framing devices and the separation of singers and protagonists, in *Mavra* the music itself draws attention to its own artificiality. Superficially, *Mavra* might seem to belong to his Russian period. But this is, in Stephen Walsh's unimprovable definition of Stravinskyan neo-classicism, 'music in which style is part of the subject matter'. It is in this sense that *Mavra* is the natural successor to *Pulcinella* and can be seen as Stravinsky's first fully-fledged neo-classical work.

The first performance of *Mavra* was given by Diaghilev's company on 3 June 1922, a couple of weeks after their première of the long-dormant *Renard*. It was a failure. Certainly mis-staged – in a rare lapse of theatrical judgement Diaghilev had presented this most domestically-scaled of operas in the vast space of the Paris Opera House, sandwiched between *Petrushka* and *The Rite of Spring* – it was also widely misunderstood. There was puzzlement as to what Stravinsky meant by it, and irritation at what must have seemed another wilful change of direction by a composer already becoming a watchword for unpredictability. (As one journalist put it a couple of years later: 'Even if his admirers know where he comes from and where he is at the moment, they have no idea where he's going.') This reaction to a piece for which he had a particular soft spot clearly rankled with Stravinsky; there are few works about which he waxes so polemical so often in his later publications. But at the same time, as he reports in his *Autobiography*, 'I was glad to see that I had completely succeeded in realising my musical ideas, and was therefore encouraged to develop them further.' The work he now began to compose was the *Octet* for wind instruments.

It was at around this time that Stravinsky told his wife about Vera Sudeikina. There was evidently a painful scene, which the composer reported to Vera in a letter she destroyed at his request. He told Catherine that he was in love with Vera, and she with him, and that he could not live without her. Furthermore, he expected Catherine to accept the situation and wanted her to make friends with Vera herself. Amazingly, this seems to be precisely what happened. At his instigation, the two women met in 1925 when Stravinsky was on tour in the United States, and a genuine affection seems to have grown up between them. 'If there has to be another woman, I am glad that it is you,' Catherine told her rival. More remarkably still, she never failed to enquire solicitously after Vera in letters to her husband, even when she herself was in the final stages of tuberculosis; and Vera, who often received letters sooner than Catherine from Stravinsky's tours, would regularly contact her to pass on his news. (Vera's husband's reaction, by contrast, was at quite the other extreme. In November 1921 Stravinsky was in London for the première of *The Sleeping Beauty*, in which Vera played the mime part of the Queen. On his return to Paris he had a blazing encounter with Sudeikin, who threatened to kill his wife for her infidelity. In August, Sudeikin left for America, never to return.) It is impossible to know what anguish underlay the apparently even surface of this triangular relationship, which was to define Stravinsky's domestic arrangements until Catherine's death 17 years later, but there can be no doubt that, as all who knew the couple have attested, Vera remained at the emotional centre of the composer's life to the very end.

What Robert Craft has succinctly called Stravinsky's 'marital dualism' was soon an open secret in his circle, and he took the opportunity of appearing in public with Vera whenever decorum permitted. There was one person, however, from whom he was at great pains to conceal the relationship. This was his mother, Anna, who was about to re-enter his life. Ever since the 1917 Revolution, Stravinsky had been negotiating to get her out of Russia, initially with Arthur Lourié, the commissar of music in what was now Petrograd, who was himself to emigrate to the West and became the composer's musical assistant for much of the inter-war period. Eventually, in 1922, Anna was given permission to leave and made her way across the Baltic to Stettin. It was a condition of her entry to Europe that her son should meet her off the boat, and since there were many delays during the course of the journey, Stravinsky found himself killing time in Berlin for some weeks during the autumn. Part of this time was spent in the company of the young American composer George Antheil, who has left some colourful, if unreliable, accounts of the composer during these weeks. When Anna finally arrived in November, she soon demonstrated that, at 68, she had lost none of her ability to infuriate her son: before they had even left Berlin, according to Antheil, they had had a row about the musical merits of Scriabin which reduced Stravinsky almost to tears. By the end of the month, she was installed with the family in Biarritz, increasing still further the number of Stravinsky's dependants, and for the remaining years of her life he seems to have lived in permanent terror of her finding out about Vera.

Meanwhile, Stravinsky continued to occupy the one-room studio above the Pleyel pianola factory in Paris, where Cocteau and the Russian poet Mayakovsky visited him around this time. Cocteau has left a vivid description of the meeting, at which the composer acted as interpreter between the two visitors, like someone 'engaged on a strange sort of smuggling adventure, traveling all alone from one tongue to the other, and only letting through what he chose to let through'. He also described Stravinsky as like 'an animal in its carapace', surrounded by pianos, drums, metronomes, cymbals and an array of his personal possessions, and observed with awe the orderliness of his working procedures, which was noted by friends and collaborators throughout his career. 'Stravinsky's order is terrifying,' he wrote. 'It recalls the surgeon's instrument case.' Mayakovsky remembered 'the soul-searching wail of pianolas being tested', which floated up to 'the composer's tiny upstairs room... crowded with pianos and pianolas.' 'He speaks rapturously of the pianola,' he wrote, 'of composing for eight, for sixteen, even for twenty-two hands!'

This was indeed the period of Stravinsky's love affair with the mechanical piano. In 1920, he had signed a lucrative contract with the Pleyel company to transcribe all his works for pianola – the studio came with the deal – and for the next six years he devoted much of his time to the task. He had been aware of the pianola for many years; the Ballets Russes seem to have used pianola arrangements as early as 1912. He had delighted in its capacity to recreate the tinniness of the 'rattletrap orchestrinas' he had heard in Spain when he wrote his *Study* for the instrument in 1917, and was fascinated by what he saw as its 'unlimited possibilities of precision, velocity, and polyphony'. He would later describe the time and effort put into these transcriptions as 'forgotten exercises to no purpose, [which] represented hundreds of hours of work', but they were of enormous importance to him in the early 1920s. In particular, he seems to have seen in the mechanical piano the same promise he was later to see in recording technology: the opportunity to bequeath to posterity a definitive version of his works which would be immune to the distortions of interpreters.

The percussive background music of the Maison Pleyel may well have contributed to the final instrumentation of *The Wedding*, which came to him with the force of revelation in 1922. Once he had realised that an ensemble of four pianos and percussion would supply all his musical and dramatic needs, work was resumed apace and the final score was completed in Monaco at the beginning of April 1923. On 13 June that year, *The Wedding* finally received its first performance, more than a decade after it was conceived. Francis Poulenc was one of the

Stravinsky in 1926

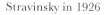

pianists at the première, which took place at the Théâtre de la Gaieté Lyrique in Paris under Ernest Ansermet. The costumes and sets were by Goncharova and the choreography by Nijinsky's sister, Bronislava Nijinska. The work was a tremendous success, which Stravinsky celebrated a few days later at an all-night party on a barge on the Seine.

In August, he travelled to Weimar for a performance of *The Soldier's Tale*, attended by the composer Ferruccio Busoni, whom Stravinsky described as having 'the noblest, most beautiful head' he had ever seen. Back in Paris, on 18 October, Stravinsky conducted the first performance of his new *Octet*, which he had completed in May. This was the first time he had presented one of his new works in public himself, and the reception was mixed. Once again, the cavernousness of the Paris Opera House was partly to blame; the tiny group of instrumentalists were lost on the stage. The programming was also bizarre, the *Octet* being followed by, of all things, a performance of Beethoven's *Eroica* symphony under Koussevitzky.

Stravinsky gave variant accounts of the origin of the *Octet*. In the most picturesque of them, he claimed it was inspired by a dream in which he found himself in a room surrounded by a small group of instrumentalists playing some attractive music. He didn't recognise the music and couldn't recall any of it the next day, but he made a point of counting the musicians – eight – and noting their instruments: two bassoons, two trombones, two trumpets, a flute and a clarinet. He awoke in delight and anticipation and began to compose the *Octet* the next morning. Whatever its inspiration, the piece, which was privately dedicated to Vera, is one of his most genial, even ebullient creations. In its three-movement structure – the first in sonata form, complete with slow introduction, the second a set of variations – it confirms, more conspicuously than *Mavra*, the neo-classical direction his music was now taking. This is the eighteenth century refracted through the prism of the twentieth, a witty fusion of classical gestures and modern sensibility. Whereas *Mavra* was its own manifesto, Stravinsky appended to the *Octet* an extended commentary on its purpose and procedures – 'Some Ideas about my Octuor' – which was published in January 1924. Beginning with the lapidary statement 'My Octuor is a musical object', this was Stravinsky's first sustained attempt to explain one of his own works in print, and it is hard not to sense in the solemn obscurity of many of its passages his lack of practice – soon remedied over the coming years – in handling the language of aesthetic self-justification. There is a world of difference between the sparks struck from his later dialogues with Robert Craft, which can illuminate whole phases of his work in a sentence, and (even allowing for translationese) such clanking periods as these:

'The aim I sought in this Octuor, which is also the aim I sought with the greatest energy in all my recent works, is to realise a musical composition through means which are emotive in themselves. These emotive means are manifested in the rendition by the heterogeneous play of movements and volumes.'

Stravinsky was later to say that he hated writing about his compositions ('How misleading are all literary descriptions of musical form'). Certainly, one would never guess from 'Some Ideas' the effervescent charm of the music it purports to describe.

If the first airing of the *Octet* was no sensation, Stravinsky seems nonetheless to have been satisfied with his performance, and from now until the late 1950s he was to give the premières of almost all his new works himself. Indeed, from 1924 he began to carve out a peripatetic career as conductor and pianist which was to transform the pattern of his working life, not to mention his earnings. As early as January of that year, he directed his *Octet*, *Mavra*, the 1919 *Firebird* suite, the *Three Pieces* and the *Concertino* for string quartet and the *Pribaoutki* at a concert in Brussels, and in March he undertook a short Spanish tour. In May, he launched another new work, his *Concerto for Piano and Wind Instruments*. This performance, under Koussevitzky's baton at the Paris Opera House, marked his first appearance as concert pianist and was not without hitch. At the end of the first movement there was a long pause before the second. Years later, Stravinsky admitted that his mind had gone a complete blank and only Koussevitky's surreptitious humming of the opening notes of the Largo had got him started again! Similar lapses occurred in later performances too – once when Stravinsky suddenly became obsessed with the idea that the audience was 'a collection of dolls in a giant panopticon'; and again when he was distracted by the reflection of his own fingers in the varnished wood of the keyboard frame.

The *Concerto* was the first of a series of works for piano, with or without instrumental accompaniment, which Stravinsky wrote specifically for his own use over the coming years, and between 1924 and 1929 he retained the exclusive performance rights, playing it more than 40 times in public. If the classicism of the *Octet* was that of Mozart and Haydn, here it is predominantly that of Bach and Handel. The work opens with a slow introductory processional of neo-Baroque dotted rhythms, and toccata figuration is to the fore throughout the outer movements. But, central though it was to the composer's repertoire, there is an unevenness to the *Concerto*, most conspicuous perhaps in the romantic swell of the second movement which seems almost to belong to another work. (Indeed, Stravinsky apparently began an entirely different slow movement for the *Concerto*, which he lost and could never subsequently remember.)

It has often been remarked that, while Stravinsky invariably composed at the piano – 'Fingers are not to be despised,' he once wrote, 'they are great inspirers, and, in contact with a musical instrument, often give birth to subconscious ideas which might otherwise never come to life'– his writing for the instrument itself is not always comfortable. This is true to a lesser extent of the work he wrote immediately after the *Concerto*, the *Sonata* for piano. Like the *Octet* and the *Concerto*, the *Sonata* is in three movements on the fast-slow-fast classical pattern. It belongs to the period of Stravinsky's rediscovery of Beethoven, a composer he had told Proust he detested only two years before, but whom he now regarded, in a characteristically Stravinskyan phrase, as 'a tremendous constructive force'. The influence of the German master can be felt throughout, though the Baroque is never far away, perhaps most especially (despite the composer's own description of it as 'Beethoven *frisé*') in the elaborately decorated lines of the Adagietto. Prokofiev, who heard the *Sonata* in Venice in 1925, was perceptive, if uncharitable, when he dubbed it 'Bach but with pockmarks'.

Stravinsky claimed that his use of the term 'sonata' was intended not to connote the classical form but to reclaim the word's original derivation, from 'sonare' ('to sound') as against 'cantare' ('to sing'). The distinction no doubt reflects an attribute of Stravinsky's own piano technique, the electrifying effect of which was noted by so many witnesses. He was no virtuoso – the *Three Pieces from Petrushka*, for example, were quite beyond him – but he possessed, in the American composer Elliot Carter's words, a 'very telling quality of attack... embodying often in just one sound the very quality so characteristic of his music – incisive but not brutal, rhythmically highly controlled yet filled with intensity so that each note was made to seem weighty and important.'

During the writing of the *Sonata*, the Stravinskys moved from Biarritz to Nice, where they installed themselves in the Villa des Roses, 167 Boulevard Carnot, and where all four of

The composer at the keyboard, in Cocteau's caricature of Stravinsky rehearsing *The Rite of Spring*

his children went down with diphtheria. The *Sonata* was finished in October, after which the composer set off on a concert tour which took in Warsaw, Prague, Leipzig, Berlin, Amsterdam, the Hague, Geneva, Lausanne and Marseilles. Then, at the end of the year, he embarked on his most significant tour to date.

Stravinsky's music had been well received in the United States during Diaghilev's 1916 seasons, but Stravinsky himself had stayed (grudgingly) in Europe. Now he judged it time to take his work to the New World in person. On 27 December 1924, he sailed for New York on the *SS Paris*. It was not only the beginning of the most profitable concert tour of his life; it was also the start of a relationship with the country which would soon be providing some of his most important commissions and which, 15 years later, he would make his permanent home.

Between January and March 1925, Stravinsky presented his work as conductor or pianist in New York, Boston, Philadelphia, Cleveland, Chicago, Detroit and Cincinnati in programmes which included not only the *Concerto*, but also the *Firebird* suite, *Fireworks*, the *Scherzo fantastique*, *The Song of the Nightingale*, and the concert suite he had made from *Pulcinella*. He was interviewed wherever he went, demonstrating from the moment of disembarkation (when he proclaimed his detestation of modern music!) the *ex cathedra* controversialism which had characterised his public pronouncements ever since *The Firebird*. A journalist who sat in on one of his rehearsals likened him to an electric shock and described the instantly galvanising effect of his arrival: 'a metallic insect all swathed in hat, spectacles, muffler, overcoat, spats, and walking stick; and accompanied by three or four secretarial, managerial personages... In a minute, business was upon the entire assemblage.' The same interviewer later elicited from Stravinsky the famous statement: 'What interests me most of all is construction. What gives me pleasure is to see how much of my material I can get into line. I want to see what is coming. I am interested first in the melody, and the volumes, and the instrumental sounds, and the rhythm.' In another exchange, on the perennial allegation of lack of emotion in his music, Stravinsky adroitly turned the tables on his interlocutor:

"'Suppose you went out and narrowly escaped being run over by a trolley car. Would you have an emotion?"

"I should hope so, Mr Stravinsky."

"So should I. But if I went out and narrowly escaped being run over by a trolley car, I would not immediately rush for some music paper and try to make something out of the emotion I had just felt.'"

There could be no better gloss on his later, notorious and much misunderstood dictum: 'music is, by its very nature, essentially powerless to *express* anything at all.'

It was during this American tour that Catherine and Vera, back in Nice, met one another for the first time. In an equally uncomfortable mirror-image of that meeting, Stravinsky himself had a very public close encounter with Serge Sudeikin on the stage of the Metropolitan Opera House in New York in the final days of his tour. Sudeikin had designed the sets for a performance of *Petrushka*, which was attended by the composer. At the end of the performance, Stravinsky was called to the stage, but as he walked on saw Sudeikin approaching from the opposite wings. The composer stopped in his tracks, gave a quick bow and turned on his heel, thus arousing the suspicions of the press, who soon unearthed the story. (As the abdication crisis was to show a decade later, in that pre-televisual age the American and European press still occupied hermetically sealed compartments, and Anna Stravinsky's ignorance of her son's double life remained blissfully undisturbed.)

No sooner had he returned home than he set off again, this time to Barcelona and shortly afterwards to Rome. In September, he was in Venice with Vera for the festival of the International Society for Contemporary Music, staying at the palazzo of his friend the Princess de Polignac, where one witness described 'the fine flower of international snob society' hanging on his every word. While there he suffered from a suppurating abscess on his forefinger which he feared might prevent him from playing his *Sonata*, scheduled at the Teatro La Fenice on 8 September. On the night of the concert, he begged the audience's indulgence, but when he sat down to the keyboard and removed the plaster on his finger he found that it had 'miraculously' healed – a cure he attributed to the power of prayer.

Schoenberg was also in Venice for the festival; his *Serenade* was performed the same day as Stravinsky's *Sonata*. The two composers seem not to have been on speaking terms at the time and didn't meet. In America Stravinsky had expatiated on Schoenberg's 'grotesque errors'; Schoenberg for his part despised the direction Stravinsky was taking in such works as the *Octet*, the *Concerto* and the *Sonata*. The depth of the

'More a chemist of music than an artistic creator': Arnold Schoenberg (1874-1951). Relations between the two composers were notoriously cool.

animosity can be judged from the words of one of Schoenberg's *Three Satires*, composed shortly after the Venice festival:

'Why, who's coming here?
It's little Modernsky!
He's had his hair cut in an old-fashioned queue,
And it looks quite nice,
Like real false hair –
Like a wig –
Just like (at least little Modernsky thinks so)
Just like Father Bach!'

It is indicative of the new pace of Stravinsky's life that only one of his compositions bears the date 1925, the *Serenade in A* for piano, the first performance of which was given by the composer at a concert in Frankfurt on 25 November. Perhaps his most rounded work for solo piano, the *Serenade* resulted from discussions with a recording company during his American tour and was designed so that each movement could fit neatly onto one side of a 78 rpm gramophone record. His first American commission, it is thus also one of the earliest works composed specifically for recording. Stravinsky described it as an imitation of a classical *Nachtmusik* and later described its four movements (with little support from the music) in terms of the phases of an eighteenth-century evening's musical entertainment. They are designated 'Hymne', 'Romanza', 'Rondoletto' and 'Cadenza Finale', each beginning and ending with the A of the title, which Stravinsky described not as the work's tonality but as the 'axis of sound' around which the music revolves. The *Serenade* is his first major piece of piano writing since the student *Sonata in F Sharp Minor* not to concern itself principally with the instrument's percussive qualities. Indeed, there is a romantic tendency to some of the harmony (albeit kept on a short rein in the composer's own 1934 recording) which could be read as a reaction to the 'errors' he accused Schoenberg of committing in his attempt to 'escape from romanticism'. The *Serenade* is dedicated to Catherine.

The day after its première, Stravinsky and Vera travelled to Copenhagen for a 10-day concert tour, from which they returned to Paris on 7 December. Five days later, Stravinsky got his driving licence and in January 1926 bought his first car, thus initiating what he called his 'automobile phase' (in contrast to his Swiss 'bicycle phase'). Motoring excursions seem to have been one of the few entertainments he permitted to impinge on his limited composing time over the next few years.

To 1926 too belongs Stravinsky's first sacred work, always excepting the mystical *Zvezdoliki* of 1913. This is a brief Slavonic setting of the Lord's Prayer, the *Pater noster*, for *a cappella* mixed choir. The first of three short sacred choruses – he composed a *Credo* in 1932 and an *Ave Maria* two years later – the *Pater noster* bears witness to a profound change in Stravinsky's spiritual life in the mid-1920s. Baptised into the Russian Orthodox church in the Nikolsky Cathedral in St Petersburg, the young Stravinsky had been raised in the faith, but his adolescent rebellion against his upbringing had naturally included religion among its targets, and by 1900 he was no longer a practising Christian. Sometime after he left Switzerland, however, he began to re-read the Gospels and to explore other religious literature, and in April 1926, after a profound but obscure revelation at the shrine of St Anthony in Padua, he formally returned to the faith, becoming a communicant of the Russian Church in Nice. His new-found devotion was mirrored in every aspect of his life. His confessor, a priest by the name of Father Nicholas Podossenov, seems to have become virtually a member of the Nice household at around this time, and Catherine's letters to her husband are full of reminders to religious observance. Visitors to the composer's homes were often surprised to find icons of the Virgin Mary with a candle burning in front them, and other observers noted his practice of crossing himself before and after concerts. Stravinsky's scores and even his sketchbooks contain numerous drawings of the Russian cross. There can be no doubt that he meant to be taken literally when, late in life, he said: 'I regard my talents as God-given, and I have always prayed to Him for strength to use them.'

Religious feeling imbues the score of the great secular work on which Stravinsky was engaged during 1926 – the opera-oratorio *Oedipus Rex*. He wanted to write something to mark the twentieth anniversary of Diaghilev's first Paris season of 1907, and in October 1925 invited Jean Cocteau to collaborate on a version of Sophocles' tragedy, which he saw as 'the archetypal drama of purification'. For some years, Stravinsky tells us in *Dialogues*, he had felt the need to compose a large-scale dramatic work, but had been perplexed by the question of language. Russian, 'the exiled language of my heart', was an alien tongue to the vast majority of his listeners; while French, German and Italian, which were the common heritage of his European audiences, were temperamentally alien to him. In September 1925, he found a solution in a book he had picked up in Genoa on his way home from the 'miraculous' concert in Venice. This was a biography of St Francis of Assisi, from which he learnt that the saint used Provençal, his adopted tongue, for all sacred transactions, in

Stravinsky in the Pleyel factory studio, Paris, which he occupied throughout the 1920s

place of his everyday language, Italian. It was a moment of sudden illumination. 'To this reading', he wrote, 'I owe the formulation of an idea that had occurred to me often since I became *déraciné*. The idea was that a text for music might be endowed with a certain monumental character by translation backwards, so to speak, from a secular to a sacred language...' So it was that Stravinsky came to settle on Latin for the libretto of *Oedipus Rex*. In January 1926, he formally agreed terms of collaboration with Cocteau and made his first sketches for the music. Cocteau, who had recently recast another ancient myth in his *Antigone*, had already begun drafting the book in French (the Latin translation was done by a 20-year-old Sorbonne student, Jean Daniélou) and now started planning the *mise en scène* with Stravinsky's son Theodore. Characteristically, Stravinsky began to visualise the staging of the work from the moment he put pen to paper: this was to be a drama of 'living statues', in which the protagonists would address themselves directly and exclusively to the audience, and the chorus would remain faceless and immobile throughout.

In his *Autobiography*, Stravinsky skimmed over the difficulties of his collaboration with Cocteau. These were partly aesthetic (Stravinsky rejected Cocteau's first two attempts) and partly practical: the composer was often away from Paris, his 1926 itinerary taking him to Amsterdam (where he conducted his first *Rite of Spring*), Rotterdam, Haarlem, Budapest, Vienna, Zagreb, Milan, and London (where he attended the English première of *The Wedding*), as well as furnishing him with his first experience of flying. A final version of the text was eventually hammered out, however, in which the sung Latin is introduced by a series of passages in vernacular French, delivered by the Speaker – a device Stravinsky later dismissed as a 'disturbing series of interruptions' but recognised as essential to the pacing of the music. These interludes have the deliberate effect of neutralising the dramatic impact of the story by forestalling it. The listener is thus placed in the position of one of Sophocles' original audience, who would already have known the story well enough to be able to focus instead on its handling and significance (though in fact Cocteau's text leaves out facts essential to an understanding of the narrative and even prepares the audience for events which don't transpire).

Cocteau, Picasso, Stravinsky and Olga Picasso in Juan-les-Pins, Summer 1925

Stage design by Theodore
Stravinsky for his father's
Oedipus Rex

There were practical difficulties in the way of performance too. For one thing, the fact that it was to be a surprise present meant that Diaghilev had to be kept in the dark until the last minute, by which time it was too late to mount a staged production in the summer as Stravinsky and Cocteau had hoped. It was also an uphill struggle to get the production financed at such short notice. For its public première, which took place under Stravinsky's baton at the Théâtre Sarah-Bernhardt in Paris on 30 May 1927, *Oedipus Rex* was therefore given in a concert performance. The work aroused the enthusiasm of a handful of musicians, including Poulenc and Ravel, but the general reaction ranged from indifference, through puzzlement to outright hostility (notably from Schoenberg). Even Diaghilev found it 'a very macabre gift'.

What made this undoubted masterpiece of twentieth-century music so hard to understand? Perhaps it was the lack of staging, though it was little better received in its first staged performances in Vienna and Berlin in 1928. Perhaps it was the programming: arguably Stravinsky's most austere score to date, it shared a platform with one of his most luxuriant, *The Firebird*. Perhaps above all it was the barrier of style – a barrier already hinted at in the work's hybrid appellation 'opera-oratorio'. Stravinsky himself likened the score to a '*Merzbild*' (a Dada term for a picture made up of rubbish) and elements of its stylistic mix can still seem incongruous today. The Folies Bergères jauntiness of Creon's aria ('Respondit deus'), for example, or the chorus' manic tarantella 'Mulier in vestibulo', have often raised listeners' eyebrows. Binding these disparate elements together, though, is a profound unity of conception and purpose, on which Stravinsky's quotation from Edmund Spenser – 'Soule is form, and doth the bodie make' – remains perhaps the most telling commentary.

From its opening bars, in which the chorus laments the plague afflicting Thebes as punishment for Oedipus' as yet undiscovered crime, the music of *Oedipus Rex* is pervaded by an atmosphere of menace strangely akin to religious awe. If, as oratorio, its breadth is Handelian, as opera its presiding spirit is Verdi, whose influence on the score – most strikingly in Jocasta's great Act Two aria 'Nonn'erubiskite' – Stravinsky himself was happy to acknowledge. Cocteau's liberties with Sophocles have been exhaustively detailed. For Stravinsky, however, the significance of the Oedipus myth lay not in its individual characters, but in its evocation of the power of fate, and in this his treatment is chillingly faithful to the Greek original. For all that the central roles are dramatically delineated – the undertow of uncertainty behind Oedipus' reassurances to his people is as evident in the wavering quality of his music as is Jocasta's almost sinister strength in hers – the abiding impression left by *Oedipus Rex* is of human lives helplessly in thrall to the whims of an inscrutable destiny.

As the pioneering Stravinsky scholar Eric Walter White has pointed out, *Oedipus* stands at the mid-point both of Stravinsky's creative output and of his life, and is the work in which his neo-classical phase entered its maturity. It is also the last work he wrote specifically for Diaghilev. In the years to come, the New World would play an ever increasing part in his artistic as well as in his professional life.

Part of Stravinsky's score for Act Two of *Oedipus Rex*

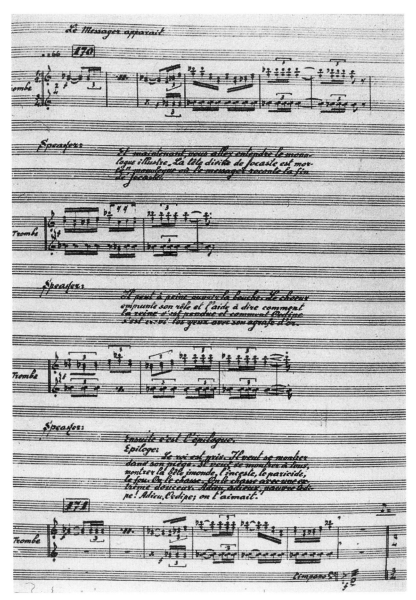

Chapter 6

Towards America (1927-1939)

A few weeks before the première of *Oedipus Rex*, Stravinsky had received his first major American commission. In April, the philanthropist and patron Elizabeth Sprague Coolidge had approached him for a 'little ballet' to be performed as part of a festival of contemporary music at the Library of Congress in Washington DC. The composer could choose his own subject: the only requirements were that the piece should last no more than half an hour and be limited to three or four dancers. 'This proposal suited me admirably,' Stravinsky wrote in his *Autobiography*, 'for... it enabled me to carry out an idea which had long tempted me, to compose a ballet founded on moments or episodes in Greek mythology plastically interpreted by dancing of the so-called classical school.'

The theme he chose was that of Apollo Musagetes (the ballet's original title, meaning 'Apollo leader of the muses', though Stravinsky came to prefer plain *Apollo*), and promptly made six of the nine classical muses redundant to meet his patron's conditions. He began working on the ballet in July 1927 and the composition was completed by the end of the year. While the Library of Congress obviously had first call on the work, Stravinsky also kept Diaghilev informed about it with a view to a European run by the Ballets Russes.

Apollo is the first of Stravinsky's 'white' or abstract ballets and bears witness to that love of classical dance which his orchestrations from *The Sleeping Beauty* had helped to reawaken. Indeed, he described it as the first attempt to revive 'academic dancing' in a work composed specifically for the purpose. The choice of subject is no coincidence. Stravinsky famously characterised creativity as an 'eternal conflict... between the Apollonian and the Dionysian principles', and in describing classical dance, as we have seen, as 'the triumph of studied conception over vagueness, of the rule over the arbitrary, of order over the haphazard', he identified it as 'the perfect expression of the Apollonian principle' in art. It was a distinction to which he reverted in his 1939-40 Harvard lectures, the *Poetics of Music*:

'What is important for the lucid ordering of the work – for its crystallisation – is that all the Dionysian elements which set the imagination of the artist in motion and make the life-sap rise must be properly subjugated before they intoxicate us, and must finally be made to submit to the law: Apollo demands it.'

The idea of the 'white ballet' informed the work from the start: 'I found the absence of many-coloured effects and of all superfluities produced a wonderful freshness', Stravinsky wrote in his *Autobiography*. 'This inspired me to write music of an analogous character.' In particular, it determined both the diatonic nature of the score and the instrumentation: after many years during which his instrumental music had been characterised by the harsher sounds of winds and percussion (including the piano), Stravinsky now returned to the strings, scoring *Apollo* for string orchestra alone. In *Dialogues*, the composer described it as his 'first attempt to compose a large-scale work in which contrasts of volumes replace contrasts of instrumental colours'.

There is nothing else quite like *Apollo* in Stravinsky's output. From the very first bars, it breathes a measured grace behind whose professed 'tribute to the French seventeenth century' the Tchaikovsky of the *Serenade for Strings* can be felt at times very close. The First Scene consists of a 'Prologue' representing Apollo's birth in music at once noble and touched with mystery. The Second Scene, which forms the rest of the ballet, begins with a *pas seul* of halting tristesse for the god, in which solo violins carry the melody, and continues with a series of classical dances for the muses and Apollo himself, of which Calliope's is modelled on the rhythm of the alexandrine, the metre of classical French poetry. The ballet concludes with an 'Apotheosis' of tranquil stateliness in which Apollo leads the muses to Parnassus.

The first performance of *Apollo* took place in the hall of the Library of Congress in Washington on 27 April 1928. Of more significance to Stravinsky's future career, though, was the European première, which he conducted at the Théâtre Sarah-Bernhardt in Paris in June. This was the occasion of his first collaboration with the choreographer George Balanchine, who was to play a crucial role in the staging of many of Stravinsky's later theatre works. Balanchine, a Russian dancer who had

Alice Nikitina and Serge Lifar
in Balanchine's 1928 production
of *Apollo*

joined Diaghilev's company as a 20-year-old in 1924, cut his choreographic teeth on Stravinsky with a version of *The Song of the Nightingale* in Paris the following year, and the composer described his collaboration with him on *Apollo* as one of the most satisfying experiences of his artistic life. For Balanchine it was a turning point in his outlook: 'In its discipline and restraint, its sustained one-ness of tone and feeling,' he later wrote, 'it was a revelation. It seemed to tell me that I could dare not to use everything, that I too could eliminate.' Balanchine emigrated to the United States in 1934, five years before Stravinsky himself, and co-founded the Ballet Society (later the New York City Ballet), through which he was to exercise an influence on the direction of modern dance comparable to that of Fokine, Nijinsky and Massine in earlier years.

Stravinsky's acceptance of the Elizabeth Sprague Coolidge commission cast another shadow over his relations with Diaghilev. Where former protégés were concerned, the great

George Balanchine (1904-1983), photographed at Covent Garden in 1950

impresario was as quick as ever to read diversification as treachery, and he inveighed against the unfortunate Mrs Coolidge in icy terms. She was completely deaf, he said; Stravinsky countered that she might be deaf but she paid; Diaghilev accused him of thinking of nothing but money (it had long been his bitter quip that the 'or' in 'Igor' stood for 'gold'). Stravinsky reserved to him the European rights to *Apollo*, but the affair still rankled with Diaghilev. For his part, Stravinsky resented the cuts Diaghilev insisted on making to one of the dances after the ballet's first performance. The composer's next commission was to cause a breach between the two men which would never be healed.

In December 1927, Stravinsky's publishers, the Edition Russe de Musique, had been approached by Diaghilev's one-time collaborator Benois on behalf of the Russian dancer and patroness Ida Rubinstein. She wanted to use *Apollo* in the repertoire of a new ballet company she was planning to launch in Paris, but Diaghilev's European performing rights made this impossible. She therefore commissioned Stravinsky to write a new work for her instead. As with the Coolidge commission, the subject and treatment would be up to him; Benois suggested, though, that he write something inspired by the music of Tchaikovsky, the thirty-fifth anniversary of whose death fell in November 1928, the month fixed for the first performance. As with *The Nightingale* 20 years earlier, Stravinsky turned to Hans Christian Andersen for his subject, this time settling on the tale of *The Ice Maiden*. The resulting ballet, *The Fairy's Kiss* (*Le Baiser de la fée*) tells the story of a young man who is marked in childhood by the kiss of a mysterious fairy. Eighteen years later, on the eve of his wedding, the fairy appears again, disguised as a gypsy at a village fair, the musical evocation of which recalls the framing scenes of *Petrushka*. She leads him to a mill, where she substitutes herself for his bride and spirits him off to her eternal domain. Here, in the final scene, to music of icy immobility, she kisses him once more, this time on the foot, claiming him for ever. Stravinsky saw in this story a (decidedly oblique) parallel to the life of Tchaikovsky himself, 'the Muse having similarly branded [him] with her fatal kiss, whose mysterious imprint made itself felt in all this great artist's work', as he put it in his dedication. To that extent, *The Fairy's Kiss* is intended as an allegory.

Once he had surfaced from a particularly busy concert schedule in May and June, in the course of which he gave *Oedipus Rex* its English première, Stravinsky devoted himself to *The Fairy's Kiss* during the summer and autumn of 1928. The family were now spending their summers at the Châlet des Echarvines, at Tailloires on the Lac d'Annécy, but Stravinsky, who could never bear to compose anywhere he could be overheard, took a room in an isolated mason's cottage for his work. This turned out to be far from the haven of peace he had hoped for. The mason went out each morning, leaving him to his music, but came home every lunchtime for a cataclysmic row with his wife, which always ended in her running out of the house with her child screaming in her arms and her husband in hot pursuit. One evening while Stravinsky was sitting on the verandah of the chalet with his sons, they heard the mason's wife screaming for help, and ran to her rescue, only to find that she and the mason had disappeared. The next day they reported the incident to the mayor, who went to investigate, whereupon 'the famous scene from Molière's *Médecin Malgré Lui* was repeated. Like Martine, the woman resolutely took her husband's part and declared that she had no reason to complain of him.' Somehow the ballet got written by the end of October. As each part of the score was finished, Stravinsky sent it to Nijinska in Paris for her to choreograph, and *The Fairy's Kiss* received its first performance by the Ida Rubinstein Company at the Paris Opera House on 27 November, with the composer conducting.

Forged as it is from a fusion of recomposed Tchaikovsky songs and piano pieces and uncannily Tchaikovskyan music of Stravinsky's own making, *The Fairy's Kiss* is in many ways one of his least characteristic scores. If *Pulcinella* is a repetition of Pergolesi in Stravinsky's own accent, *The Fairy's Kiss* is more like the creation of a third musical personality which is neither Tchaikovsky nor Stravinsky but shares some of the characteristics of both. For many, it seemed another sell-out by the one-time prince of modernism. For Diaghilev, it was the last straw. It was bad enough to pick up the European crumbs from an American commission, as he felt he had with *Apollo*; it was a thousand times worse to have Stravinsky helping a rival ballet company to compete with him in Paris. It was as if he had been betrayed by his own family, and there is a kind of tragic paternalism in the bitterness with which he savaged *The Fairy's Kiss* and its composer. 'Stravinsky, our famous Igor, my first son, has given himself up entirely to the love of God and cash,' he wrote. All relations were broken off. In June 1929 the two men found themselves in adjacent apartments in Albemarle Court in London, where Stravinsky kept a flat at this time; but although they could hear each other's voices through the wall, neither broke the silence between them. There was to be no reconciliation. On 19 August, Diaghilev died in his room at the Grand Hotel, Venice, where, in the ground-floor salon 17 years earlier, Stravinsky had first played him the 'Dances of the Adolescents' from *The Rite of Spring*. The Ballets Russes did not long survive him.

By now the pattern of Stravinsky's life as composer and performer had firmly established itself, and would remain broadly the same for the last decade of his residence in Europe. Domestically, he shuttled between Vera (in Paris) and his family (in Nice until June 1931, and thereafter in Voreppe, near Grenoble). His concert tours continued, often intensively, eating into his composing time but providing a steady source of income. Other earnings derived from the sale of his manuscripts (he later complained that he made more from his music in this form than he ever did from the works themselves) and from performance royalties, though until 1934 he received nothing from the United States, which had not signed the Berne Copyright Convention with the Soviet Union. From this time too dates his association with Columbia Records; at this stage of his career, he was seduced by the new technology and embraced the prospect it seemed to offer of laying down an authoritative version of his works. (Pieces recorded during this period have now been released on compact disc, but the greater part of his recorded legacy, further details of which are given on pages 197 to 200, dates from his work with Columbia in the 1950s and 1960s.) He also continued to receive income from commissions.

The dual needs of his performing and composing careers continued to determine what he wrote during this period too. On the performing side, the centrepiece of his piano repertoire had for the last five years been the *Concerto*. By 1929, however, when his exclusive performance rights to it came to an end, it had already done the rounds of the European and American concert circuit, and Stravinsky felt it was high time to freshen up his act. He therefore began a new piano concerto for his own use, calling it *Capriccio*, partly for stylistic reasons but perhaps principally from his deep-rooted distaste for repeating himself.

Like the *Concerto*, the *Capriccio* is in three movements on the fast-slow-fast classical model. Although it is a more genial work than its predecessor, and despite Alban Berg's double-edged compliment that he wished he could write 'such light-hearted music', it is far from the piece of musical froth its title might suggest. The first movement has its share of shadows – indeed, its mixture of musical moods often seems to strain heterogeneity to its limits – and the restraint of the slow movement is punctuated by outbreaks of darker drama derived from its opening piano figure. However, the finale, an Allegro capriccioso which was the first part of the work to be written, reclaims the fairground insouciance of the first movement's airier passages and serves briskly to dispel the lurking shades of its predecessors. A conspicuous feature of the piano writing is the use of rapid repetition of a single note, which recalls Stravinsky's cimbalom music of the immediate post-war years and would reappear in his *Duo Concertant* and the *Concerto for Two Solo Pianos*. Stravinsky gave the first performance of the *Capriccio* under the baton of Ernest Ansermet at the Salle Pleyel in Paris on 6 December 1929. Six days later, he agreed terms for the work which stands at the pinnacle of his achievement during the inter-war years – the *Symphony of Psalms*.

Like *Apollo*, this was an American commission. Around September, Stravinsky had been approached by Serge Koussevitzky for a symphonic work to mark the fiftieth anniversary of the Boston Symphony Orchestra, of which he was the conductor. Beyond the 'symphonic' tag, there were no specific requirements as to the form the work should take. As so often with Stravinsky, however, the commission served to focus ideas which had been in the back of his mind for some time. He had long wanted to write a symphonic work, he says in his *Autobiography*, but:

'Symphonic form as bequeathed to us by the nineteenth century held little attraction for me, inasmuch as it had flourished in a period the language and ideas of which were all the more foreign to us because it was the period from which we emerged. As in the case of my *Sonate* [sic], I wanted to create an organic whole without conforming to the various models adopted by custom, but still retaining the periodic order by which the symphony is distinguished from the suite...

'I also had under consideration the sound material with which to build my edifice. My idea was that my symphony should be a work with great contrapuntal development, and for that it was necessary to increase the media at my disposal. I finally decided on a choral and instrumental ensemble in which the two elements should be on an equal footing, neither of them outweighing the other.'

He had also been planning a symphonic setting of the psalms for some time, and took into account his publisher's suggestion that he write something 'popular' (!) to the extent of choosing the well-known Psalm 150 as one of his texts. The psalms are in the Latin of the Vulgate, but Stravinsky seems to have begun composing the work to the Slavonic texts he had loved from his schooldays. As usual, composition had to be fitted in between heavy concert schedules, which took him all over Europe in the first and last quarters of 1930, but the full score of the *Symphony of Psalms* was completed in August and given its first performance, not in Boston as one might have expected, but in Brussels under Ernest Ansermet, on 13 December 1930. The American première followed six days later, with Serge Koussevitzky conducting the Boston Symphony Orchestra, who found themselves in exalted company on the work's title page ('This symphony, composed to the glory of God, is dedicated to the Boston Symphony Orchestra').

The *Symphony of Psalms* is in three parts, the first of which is a cry for forgiveness ('Exaudi orationem meam'; 'Hear my prayer, O Lord'). The second is a massive double fugue on a theme which recalls that of Bach's *Musical Offering*, and is a prayer that a new song be put into the mouth of the believer. Stravinsky saw the song of the final part (Psalm 150: 'Alleluja. Laudate dominum'; 'Alleluia. Praise ye the Lord') as the answer to that prayer, and characterised the hushed reverence of its final pages – though with a touch of the embarrassment which seems also to have prevented his discussing the *religious* origins of the work – as 'the calm of praise'. The extraordinary power of this long, slow concluding ostinato derives substantially from its counter-textual restraint. Indeed, it seems almost to dramatise the tension between Stravinsky's belief in the fundamental inexpressiveness of music and the whole idea of writing a religious work in a spirit of worship: while the words speak of praising God on sounding cymbals, the music preserves the steady tread of a ritual procession. But there is no irony in that tension. Rather, it conveys a sense of potential energy, the potential energy of faith, accumulating like water behind a dam. The *Symphony of Psalms* is one of the great acts of devotion in the music of the twentieth century. As Francis Poulenc wrote after the first performance, 'It is a work of peace... One can only wonder at Stravinsky's powers of renewal.'

His autumn concert schedule took him to Berlin, Vienna, Mainz, Wiesbaden, Bremen, Munich, Nuremberg, Frankfurt and Mannheim, where the *Capriccio* was the centrepiece of most of his programmes. Mainz was also the home of the music publishers B Schott's Söhne, who had recently taken over the publication of some of his early works; and while he was there Stravinsky had discussions with one of the directors, Willy Strecker, who would be among the composer's closest associates during the 1930s. The talks touched on the possibility of his writing a violin concerto for the 39-year-old virtuoso Samuel Dushkin, who was a friend of Strecker's. Stravinsky was doubtful. He says he questioned whether his knowledge of violin technique was adequate to the task – a claim which rings somewhat hollow from the composer of *The Soldier's Tale* and a man so meticulous about mastering the practical requirements of the instruments for which he wrote that he had been known to install suites of percussion in his rooms to test their capacities. A more plausible reason for his doubts is his open distrust of virtuosi, whom he saw, like conductors, as constitutionally inclined to showmanship. Indeed, once he had met Dushkin in person, his hesitation evaporated.

Dushkin has given a vivid account of this meeting, and of his work with Stravinsky on the *Violin Concerto* (sometimes known simply as the *Concerto in D*). He found the composer, contrary to reputation, a man of great personal charm, whose capacity for giving affection was of a piece with his need to receive it. 'I sensed very soon something tense and anguished about him' Dushkin wrote, 'which made one want to comfort and reassure *him*. The Stravinsky I had heard about and imagined and the Igor Feodorovich I met seemed two different people.' Like a host of other observers throughout the composer's life – Ramuz in Switzerland during the First World War, Cocteau in Paris in the 1920s, Robert Craft in the 1950s and 1960s – Dushkin was especially impressed by the extreme orderliness of Stravinsky's working methods.

The collaboration seems to have been an unusually close and amicable one. Stravinsky would discuss the violin part with Dushkin at every opportunity. One day, over lunch in a Paris restaurant, he wrote a chord on a piece of paper and asked Dushkin if he could play it. Dushkin said it was impossible, and Stravinsky was very disappointed. When he got home, however, the violinist tried it out and found it was playable after all. The chord, which Stravinsky described as his 'passport' to the concerto, begins each of the work's four movements.

1931 started with the usual concert tours, one of which took him to Trieste, from where he travelled to Venice with Vera and laid flowers at Diaghilev's grave on the island of San Michele. In June, the family moved from Nice to the sylvan surroundings of the Château de la Vironnière, near Voreppe, where Stravinsky spent his summers up until 1935. In between times, he worked on the *Violin Concerto*, which was completed in September and given its first performance by Dushkin and the Berlin Radio Orchestra, conducted by the composer, on 23 October. Despite the mixed reception that was becoming traditional for his new works, Stravinsky clearly enjoyed working with Dushkin, with whom he immediately embarked on a European tour, performing the *Concerto* at concerts in Frankfurt, London, Cologne, Hanover and Paris. He therefore decided to produce another piece which he and Dushkin could tour together, and in December began work on the five-movement *Duo Concertant* for violin and piano, the third and final movements of which, idiosyncratically titled 'Eclogue II' and 'Dithyrambe', recall the poignant lyricism of the *Concerto*'s two central Arias. The two musicians gave the first performance of the *Duo Concertant* in Berlin on 28 October 1932 and subsequently took the work on tour in the first of a series

A programme from one of Stravinsky's concert tours with the violinist Samuel Dushkin

THE HALLÉ CONCERTS SOCIETY.
SEASON 1933-1934.

SEVENTEENTH CONCERT
Thursday Evening, February 22nd, 1934, at 7-30.

STRAVINSKY CONCERT

Artist:

Violinist - - - - - SAMUEL DUSHKIN

As a mark of respect to the late King Albert of Belgium, Chopin's "Funeral March" will be played before the commencement of the programme.

PROGRAMME
Part I.

FANTASIA—"Feuerwerk" (Op. 4) - - - - - *Stravinsky.*

"SUITE ITALIENNE" FOR VIOLIN AND PIANOFORTE
Stravinsky.
SAMUEL DUSHKIN and IGOR STRAVINSKY.

CONCERTO IN D FOR VIOLIN AND ORCHESTRA - *Stravinsky.*
SAMUEL DUSHKIN.

INTERVAL OF FIFTEEN MINUTES.

Part II.

"PASTORALE" FOR VIOLIN, WIND QUARTET AND
PIANOFORTE - - - - - - - - - *Stravinsky.*

TRANSCRIPTIONS FOR VIOLIN AND PIANOFORTE—
Les Airs du Russignol - - - - - - - *Stravinsky.*
Marche Chinoise - - - - - - - - *Stravinsky.*
Berceuse - - - - - - - - - - *Stravinsky.*
Scherzo - - - - - - - - - - *Stravinsky.*
Danse Russe - - - - - - - - - *Stravinsky.*

SUITE FROM THE BALLET—"L'Oiseau de Feu" *Stravinsky.*

Guest Conductor - IGOR STRAVINSKY.

of concerts, for which Stravinsky also made violin and piano transcriptions of some of his early works, including the *Pastorale* and the 'Russian Dance' from *Petrushka*. He continued to tour with Dushkin until 1937, periodically adding other transcriptions to their repertoire, including a violin and piano suite from *Pulcinella*, which he called *Suite italienne*.

It was in 1932 also that Stravinsky had his first encounter with Mussolini, who summoned him to the Palazzo Venezia after a concert he gave in Rome. He was taken to a long hall, where he found the dictator seated at a large desk surrounded by ugly lamps. After a brief chat about music, the dictator mentioned that he played the violin and Stravinsky bit his lip in time to avoid making a comparison with Nero! Mussolini's characteristically grandiose parting remark was 'You will come and see me the next time you are in Rome, *and I will receive you.*' (The two men met again four years later.) The encounter is a reminder of the political climate in which Stravinsky was conducting his professional life in the early 1930s. In 1932 he, Vera Sudeikina and a Jewish photographer friend of theirs, Eric Schall, were having dinner together in a restaurant in Munich when three men wearing swastika armbands entered and began to make insulting remarks about them. As the Stravinsky party hurriedly left, the Nazis attacked Schall, who might well have been killed had a fortuitous taxi not provided them with an escape route. Chillingly, when they reported the incident to the nearest magistrate, he merely shrugged it off: 'In Germany today, such things happen every minute.' A few months later, in January 1933, as Stravinsky performed his *Capriccio* in Hamburg, the papers were full of the political manoeuverings which would result, only days after the concert, in Adolf Hitler's accession to the German Chancellorship.

Benito Mussolini around the time of his first meeting with Stravinsky

S. E. Benito Mussolini

FOT. BADODI
MILANO

In that same month, Ida Rubinstein approached Stravinsky again with a new commission. This was for a 'melodrama' based on a poem by André Gide, reworking the classical myth of Persephone's descent into the underworld and the rebirth of spring. *Persephone* developed as a kind of cantata in three scenes, for speaker, tenor, mixed chorus (including children's choir), and orchestra. The speaking part of Persephone was intended for Rubinstein herself.

Stravinsky had met Gide in Switzerland during the First World War, when they had discussed the possibility of working together on a production of *Antony and Cleopatra*. In February 1933, they met again in Wiesbaden to sketch out a plan of action for *Persephone*. At first all went well, Gide recording their 'perfect agreement' in his famous journal. As the collaboration progressed, however, that agreement came under serious strain. Stravinsky began to resent Gide's attempts to direct his musical thought. Gide for his part objected to Stravinsky's characteristic disregard for the prosody of the original poem. According to the composer, Gide

'had expected the *Perséphone* text to be sung with exactly the same stresses he would use to recite it. He believed my musical purpose should be to imitate or underline the verbal pattern: I would simply have to find pitches for the syllables, since he considered he had already composed the rhythm... And, not understanding that a poet and a musician collaborate to produce *one* music, he was only horrified by the discrepancies between my music and his.'

The first time Gide heard Stravinsky play the whole work through, he merely muttered *'c'est curieux, c'est très curieux'*, and quickly made his excuses, leaving for a holiday in Sicily to recover from the shock. Thereafter, he absented himself from rehearsals and didn't attend a single performance of the work. Later, when the libretto was published, he sent Stravinsky a copy inscribed, generously enough, with the words *'en amicale communion'*; Stravinsky rebuffed the gesture with a stinging denial that Gide had demonstrated any kind of communion with him at all.

Stravinsky worked on *Persephone* throughout the summer and autumn of 1933, during which he finally moved out of his studio at the Maison Pleyel into a furnished flat in the Rue Viète, and the score was finished, in record time, at the end of January 1934. At almost an hour, *Persephone* is the longest of Stravinsky's works before his opera *The Rake's Progress*. It is also one of his most relaxed. The return of spring celebrated here could

The French novelist André Gide (1869-1951), with whom Stravinsky experienced an 'absence of rapport'

hardly be further from the violent rebirth of *The Rite*. The pagan Russianism of the earlier work has given way to a Christianised Hellenism. As the work's designation suggests, such drama as there is tends towards melodrama: the orchestral introduction to the third scene, for example, which heralds the rituals at the temple of Demeter, has the slightly tacky grandeur of the Hollywood historical epic. But the prevailing note is one of vernal lyricism. For all Gide's objections to Stravinsky's syllabic treatment of his verse, the music seems to have fallen under the softening spell of the language in this his first setting of French words since the Verlaine songs of 1910. There is an immediacy, a spontaneity to *Persephone* which at times recalls the Berlioz of *L'Enfance du*

Christ – most strikingly perhaps in the delightful lullaby '*Sur ce lit elle repose*', which Stravinsky sketched while watching Vera sleeping. Certainly, the mixture of singing and the spoken word can be an uneasy one – as it also proves in such later works as *Babel* and *A Sermon, a Narrative and a Prayer* – and some passages no doubt demand the support of stage action to register their full effect. But it remains surprising that so beguilingly accessible a work should still have a shakier foothold in the repertoire than almost anything else Stravinsky wrote in the inter-war years.

The première of *Persephone* was given at the Paris Opera House by Ida Rubinstein's company on 30 April 1934, with the composer at the rostrum. In November, he conducted the first English performance at one of the BBC Symphony concerts in the Queen's Hall, London, at which he also played the *Capriccio*.

In between these two engagements, in June 1934, Stravinsky finally became a French citizen. A quarter of a century had passed since the commission for *The Firebird* had first established his connection with the country in which he had lived for the last 14 years. Ironically, though, naturalisation came at precisely the time when his ties with France were loosening. The Paris flat to which he and his family moved at the end of the year, 125 Rue Faubourg St-Honoré, would be his last (and least happy) European address. At the same time, his links with the United States were assuming ever greater importance in his musical life. Stravinsky had been very favourably impressed by the musical vitality of the US on his first visit in 1925, and in December 1934 he embarked on a second American tour. Two days after Christmas, he and Dushkin set sail for New York on the *SS Rex* at the beginning of a three-month concert schedule that would take them all over the States.

An interview the 52-year-old Stravinsky gave to an American journalist has left a picture of the composer at this period so vivid, and so typical of descriptions of him throughout his life, that it is worth quoting at some length:

'Stravinsky... has a strange, prehistoric face – lean, bony... He's an agitated little man with the will of a giant, fine formal gestures, and a cyclonic temperament. His is an inventive, contradictory, complicated mentality bent on comprehending everything immediately and from the ground up...

'He loves to talk, has the drawing-room charm of the verbal virtuoso, and when he listens gives the perfect attention of a clockmaker hearkening to a new movement. In an argument he always takes sides and, since he ignores concession in any form, always thinks his side is right. He hates to be alone, is always at the boiling point of gaiety or despair, has a tremendous capacity for *joie de vivre*, smokes forty bad cigarettes a day, is a connoisseur of claret, which he buys in the barrel at Bordeaux and has bottled for his special use, sensually enjoys fine brandy, champagne, and foods when he isn't concerned with conscience or diet, occasionally overeats, invariably keeps all Church festivals.'

There follows the usual account of the surgical orderliness of his desk, at which he works at composition for three hours every morning, and of his manuscripts, which are described as 'museum pieces for meticulousness'.

It was during this second American tour that Stravinsky discovered the attractions of California, which hadn't figured in his 1925 itinerary. In Hollywood, which was to become his home just four years later, he visited several film studios, had a close encounter with the movie magnate Louis B Mayer, and discussed a possible collaboration with Chaplin, whose films had fascinated him in Europe.

Stravinsky returned from the States in April 1935 convinced that the American public's interest in him went beyond his status as performer and celebrity genuinely to embrace his music. The contrast with the cool reception afforded to his recent works in Europe must have been striking. If further proof were needed of the misunderstanding and neglect to which he felt he had been subjected in France, it was not long in coming. The same year, he put himself up as a candidate for the Institut de France, but was denied the status of an 'Immortal' by the convincing margin of 27 votes to five, the place going instead to his old friend Florent Schmitt. Stravinsky was perhaps all the more humiliated for feeling he had acted out of character in seeking the honours of the Academy; he was certainly keen to stress in his accounts of the affair that he had applied only under pressure from friends. The rejection deepened his growing sense of cultural isolation in his adopted country. As he wrote in his autobiography, the first volume of which was published in April 1935 as *Chroniques de ma vie*: 'I have a very distinct feeling that in the course of the last fifteen years my written work has estranged me from the great mass of my listeners... What moves and delights me leaves them indifferent, and what still interests them holds no further attraction for me.'

The *Chroniques de ma vie* (translated into English as *An Autobiography* in 1936) is the first of Stravinsky's book-length autobiographical collaborations, though in this case the collaborator, his old friend Walter Nouvel, who virtually ghosted it, remains unacknowledged. It is a determinedly reticent work, its image of the composer carefully constructed and its account of individual works sometimes wilfully misleading. What's more, as some of the quotations in the present book will already have shown, it is a strangely colourless document, its deadpan tone in striking contrast to the wit and brio of the conversation books Stravinsky produced with Robert Craft in later years. Nonetheless, even if such self-revelation as it contains must often be sought between the lines, *An Autobiography* remains essential reading for anyone interested in the first half-century of the composer's life.

Programme for the 1935
English première of *Persephone*

series **B**

WEDNESDAY 28 NOVEMBER AT 8.30

STRAVINSKY Perséphone (Mélodrame en trois parties d'André Gide)

    I. Perséphone ravie
    II. Perséphone aux Enfers
    III. Perséphone renaissante

(First performance in England by arrangement with Ida Rubinstein)
(Conducted by the Composer)

STRAVINSKY Capriccio, for Pianoforte and Orchestra

STRAVINSKY Suite, L'Oiseau de Feu

IDA RUBINSTEIN
RENE MAISON
IGOR STRAVINSKY

A Section of
THE B.B.C. CHORUS

THE B.B.C. SYMPHONY ORCHESTRA
(LEADER ARTHUR CATTERALL)

Conductors
IGOR STRAVINSKY
SIR HENRY WOOD

123

In November 1935, Stravinsky completed the *Concerto for Two Solo Pianos*, the first movement of which had been written three years earlier. This was intended as 'a vehicle for concert tours in orchestra-less cities' with his younger son Soulima, who, since his debut in 1933 with the *Capriccio*, had been developing a career as a concert pianist. Four-handed piano playing had been a staple of Stravinsky's domestic music-making since his student days with Uncle Yelachich, and he had always tried out his music four-hands at one keyboard as he composed it. While working on the *Concerto*, however, he found he could not 'hear' a *second* piano in the same way. When he resumed the piece after writing the *Duo Concertant* and *Persephone*, therefore, he commissioned the Pleyel company to construct a special double piano for him 'in the form of a small box of two tightly-wedged triangles'. With Soulima at the other keyboard, this device enabled him to 'test-hear' the *Concerto* bit by bit as he went along. Before the score was finished, however, work was interrupted once again, this time by Stravinsky's eccentric decision to have his appendix out. His elder son Theodore had just had an emergency appendectomy, and he wanted to make sure the same thing never happened to him – a logic which, if taken to its natural extreme, might have resulted in the precautionary removal of several other non-essential organs! Vera commented on Stravinsky's tendency to extend his hypochondria to others: on this occasion, in what he described as a 'surgical spree', he insisted not only that his other children had the same operation, but also that she and a number of his friends did likewise.

The *Concerto for Two Solo Pianos*, which Robert Craft has described as the most powerful of Stravinsky's compositions of the 1930s, is an intensely concentrated work in four movements, the second of which, entitled 'Notturno', pays homage to the same tradition of *Nachtmusik* which supposedly inspired the *Serenade in A*. The third (originally placed fourth) is a set of four variations on a theme which in the final ordering of the movements only appears after it's over, in the prelude of the prelude-and-fugue finale. The Stravinskys *père et fils* gave the first performance of the work at the Salle Gaveau in Paris on 21 November 1935, Igor prefacing it with a 15-minute talk which says more about his fascination with etymology than about the music itself. Certainly, the work perplexed many of its listeners. One of them, Raïssa Maritain, voiced in particularly pithy form a view of Stravinsky's music which was gaining ground in Europe and has often been heard since: 'Admirable technically, but without the slightest inwardness; it gave me no pleasure in hearing it except such as one gets from any good professional job. There is no *song* in this music. It does not proceed from any lyrical germ but only from a musical *idea*.'

The same month that the *Concerto* was first heard, Stravinsky received another major US commission in the form of a ballet for the newly formed American Ballet. The new work was to be choreographed by Balanchine, who had now moved to the States. Musical ideas for *Jeu de cartes* (*A Card Game*) began to appear in the composer's sketchbooks almost immediately, but, as so often, his accounts of the origins of the scenario are inconsistent. In *Themes and Conclusions*, he claimed to have been thinking for more than a decade about writing a ballet with playing-card costumes and a green-baize gaming-table backdrop, locating the genesis of the idea in his first impressions of a casino during one of his childhood holidays at a German spa town (presumably Bad Homburg, where his father took him to meet the 76-year-old Clara Schumann in the summer of 1895). Elsewhere, he said that the idea came to him suddenly one evening in a cab on his way to visit friends and he was so delighted that he stopped the driver and invited him for a drink. Whatever the truth, *Jeu de cartes* took shape around the idea of a game of poker, then one of Stravinsky's favourite pastimes. The dancers represent cards and the work is divided into three 'deals', each prefaced by a clean-cut brass fanfare supposedly imitating the dealer's call '*Ein neues Spiel, ein neues Glück*'. The action is complicated by the machinations of the principal dancer – the Joker, a wild card reminiscent of Stravinsky himself in his ability to assume the identity of any other card in the pack. (Indeed, the composer looks Mephistophelean enough for the part in the ballet's official publicity shot – a rare photograph of him actually grinning!) The music of *Jeu de cartes* is shot through with allusions amounting in places to virtual quotation – most conspicuously from the overture to Rossini's *Barber of Seville* in the Third Deal. Stravinsky also quotes from his own early *Symphony in E Flat*.

The composer had a particularly heavy concert schedule in the first half of 1936. He was in Spain in March (where he shared a railway compartment from Madrid to Barcelona with Salvador Dali). Then in April he embarked on a two-month tour of South America, during which he visited Montevideo, Buenos Aires and Rio de Janeiro, performing several works, including *The Firebird*, *Persephone*, *The Fairy's Kiss* and, with Soulima, the *Concerto for Two Pianos*. As a result, *Jeu de cartes* was not completed until December, only days before he sailed for New York at the start of his third American tour. This included

A scene from the first production of *Jeu de cartes* at the Metropolitan Opera House, New York, in 1937

engagements in Toronto, New York, Washington, Detroit and Cleveland, among other smaller centres. He also visited the West Coast again, renewing his acquaintance with Hollywood and with Chaplin, and discovering (amazing as it may seem from the smog-ridden perspective of the present-day) that the invigorating cleanliness of the Los Angeles air relieved his respiratory problems. (This was to be a key factor in his later decision to make his home there, since it was during the 1937 tour that a New York doctor found ominous evidence of active tuberculosis.) Despite his busy schedule, he found time to complete a little *Praeludium* for jazz ensemble, which he had begun in Paris. The climax of the tour was the première of *Jeu de cartes* at the Metropolitan Opera House in New York on 27 April 1937, which he conducted himself. Balanchine's staging of the new ballet shared the programme with a revival of his 1928 *Apollo* and a newly choreographed version of *The Fairy's Kiss*. A week later Stravinsky sailed for home on the *SS Paris*.

With the benefit of hindsight, the events of the two years following his return from this tour seem to accelerate inexorably towards a break with Europe. As we have seen, Stravinsky's musical centre of gravity was shifting ever more decisively towards the United States, not only because audiences there showed more enthusiasm for his recent works than their European counterparts, but also because it was by now his principal source of new commissions. The work to which he devoted himself on his return to France, for example, originated in America. During the 1937 tour, Mr and Mrs Robert Woods Bliss, the first couple of Georgetown, had commissioned a concerto for chamber orchestra to celebrate their thirtieth wedding anniversary. This predominantly sunny work, the *Concerto in E Flat*, is a latter-day concerto grosso, openly modelled on Bach's Brandenburg Concertos, with the third of which its opening theme has obvious affinities. The concerto is popularly known as 'Dumbarton Oaks' after the Blisses' Georgetown house, later the scene of a famous post-war economic conference. It was completed in March 1938 and first performed there in May of the same year under the baton of Stravinsky's influential friend and advocate Nadia Boulanger.

Mrs Mildred Bliss was also the source of a second major commission in 1938, this time for a symphony destined to mark the fiftieth anniversary of the Chicago Symphony Orchestra's first concert season. But this work, the *Symphony in C*, was to have a longer and more troubled gestation than the 'Dumbarton Oaks' *Concerto*; for the years 1938 and 1939 were to be the most tragic of Stravinsky's life.

Tuberculosis had hung like a curse over his family since childhood, but it was in the 1930s that it wrought its greatest ravages. His wife Catherine had spent time in a sanatorium in Leysin after the birth of her daughter Milène in 1914, but from early in 1935 she had been confined to a sanatorium at Sancellemoz in Haute Savoie, where both her daughters, Milène and Lyudmila ('Mika') were in due course to join her. Catherine's letters to her husband, never failing in their concern for his minor ailments nor faltering in the face of her own incurable one, make painful reading during this period. Apparently still devoted to him, she never ceased to miss him during his long absences – between January and June 1936, for example, she saw him for only three days – and the loneliness of separation is as palpable in her correspondence as the horrors of her disease. But a worse trial was to follow. Her elder daughter Lyudmila had married in 1935, but in the light of the Stravinskys' medical history had been warned not to have children for three years. She gave birth to a daughter 15 months later, however, and by 1937 was also a patient at Sancellemoz. During 1938 her condition deteriorated sharply, and in November, while her father, whom one can only assume had failed to grasp the seriousness of the situation, travelled to Turin for a concert engagement, she died at the age of just 30.

Lyudmila had been a favourite daughter, and Stravinsky's grief was profound. The tragedy also led to a grave worsening of Catherine's already shattered health. On 1 February 1939, Stravinsky wrote to Willy Strecker that she was now too weak to leave her bed. 'What can I do? I wait, I hope, and I am full of anguish… A huge discouragement strikes me every hour, every day. I wait, I wait, I wait.' Just four weeks later, on 2 March, Catherine died at Sancellemoz. She was 58.

Stravinsky, who had moved to the sanatorium shortly before Catherine's death, spent the next few months as a patient there himself. It was at Sancellemoz that he worked on the second movement of the *Symphony in C*, and here too, in June, that his mother Anna died. Whereas Stravinsky seems to have grown closer to his father during the latter's final days, there had been no thawing in relations between Anna and her son. Indeed, it was only at Vera Sudeikina's insistence that he even agreed to attend her funeral – the third for a member of his family in just seven months.

Equally grim was the political situation in Europe. Civil war was raging in Stravinsky's beloved Spain, and as he was putting the finishing touches to the 'Dumbarton Oaks' *Concerto*, Hitler's troops had marched into Austria. The autumn of 1938 saw that last throw of the dice for peace, the Munich crisis, and in the month of Lyudmila's death Jews and Jewish property were attacked throughout the Reich in the notorious pogroms of *Kristallnacht*. On 1 September 1939, while Stravinsky was still living at Sancellemoz, the tanks of the *Wehrmacht* stormed into Poland, and two days later Britain and France declared war on Germany. Within hours, Stravinsky and Vera left Sancellemoz for Paris. The reality of war made itself felt almost immediately, as an air-raid warning sent them scuttling down to the basement of Vera's flat.

It is hardly surprising that Stravinsky was, in Vera's words, 'in a terrible state of nerves', a description borne out by his publisher Gavril Païchadze, who found him 'perplexed and jittery'. 'He could neither eat nor sleep,' Païchadze wrote, 'he could not work... he got angry, nervous and irritable. All he wanted was to get out as quickly as possible, out of Paris, out of Europe, into America where life was still orderly.' Craft was to speak of a 'powerful compulsion for order' as one of Stravinsky's defining characteristics. The deaths in his family, the fracturing of long-standing friendships (he quarrelled with both Arthur Lourié and Ernest Ansermet at around this time), the decline in his musical fortunes in Europe, the descent into war – numerous circumstances conspired to mark the late 1930s as the end of another phase in Stravinsky's life. But it was, above all else, that need for order which was now to determine his course of action.

For some months, Stravinsky had had a further visit to the States in his diary. In the wake of his successful 1937 tour, he had received another important American commission. This time it was not for a musical work, but for a series of six public lectures on music to be given at Harvard under the auspices of the Charles Eliot Norton Professorship of Poetry, which he had been offered for the academic year 1939-40. As with so many of his publications, the lectures, which he entitled *Poetics of Music* and which were later issued in book form, were a collaborative effort. In this case the collaborator was his friend the French composer Roland-Manuel, who largely ghosted the talks from Stravinsky's notes after discussions with him at Sancellemoz. The first of the lectures was scheduled for 18 October 1939.

In 1914, events had turned a temporary move to Switzerland into a quarter of a century's exile in Europe. On 25 September 1939, with the continent once more collapsing into war, Stravinsky embarked for New York on the *SS Manhattan*. He expected to be gone for a few months. In the event, America was to become his home for the rest of his life.

Chapter 7

A double emigré (1939-1945)

Stravinsky arrived in New York on 30 September 1939. We do not know at what stage he decided to make America his permanent home – it may already have been in the back of his mind – but certainly within a few weeks of his arrival his intention was plain. At the age of 57, he found himself, for the second time in his life, translated to an alien culture, albeit, as with Europe in 1914, one with which he already had strong artistic and social links. As he wrote late in life: 'I am a double emigré, born to a minor musical tradition and twice transplanted to other minor ones.'

He went straight from New York to Cambridge, Massachusetts, where he stayed for the next two months at Gerry's Landing, the home of Edward Forbes, the grandson of Ralph Waldo Emerson. On 18 October, in an atmosphere of great expectancy, he gave the first of his *Poetics of Music* lectures (in French) to a crowded hall at Harvard. The cream of Boston society turned out to hear him. The *Poetics*, consisting of six lectures and an epilogue, rehearse, in prose of a somewhat self-consciously academic cast, the aesthetic views of Stravinsky's French years. After the introductory 'Getting acquainted', the lectures cover 'The phenomenon of music', 'The composition of music', 'Musical typology', 'The avatars of Russian music' (a scathing rejection of the Soviet school of music, which proved the most quotably controversial of the set), and 'The performance of music'. They continued until May 1940. In addition to the lectures, the professorship of poetry entailed regular informal sessions with students, at which Stravinsky would hear and criticise their compositions, a process he seems to have enjoyed more than the lectures themselves.

He also had a number of concert engagements scheduled, and at the end of the year conducted in Boston, New York, San Francisco and Los Angeles. In the latter city, he visited the Disney studios with George Balanchine to see a screening of

Fantasia, in which a doctored version of *The Rite of Spring* accompanies animated images of the formation of the earth, the origins of life and the rise and fall of the dinosaurs. Ominously, when Stravinsky was asked if he wanted a score and replied that he had his own, he was told 'But it is all changed.' His reaction can be imagined. It was a salutary introduction to the ways of the Hollywood movie industry, with which, despite his own insatiable appetite for movie-going, his relations were to be at best ambiguous over the coming years. (It is typical of Stravinsky's view of his art that when someone suggested that *Fantasia* would bring his music to the attention of a wider public, he responded that he was interested not in the quantity of his listeners but in 'the quality of listening, the quality of the individual soul'.)

Stravinsky spent the New Year period with Mr and Mrs Robert Woods Bliss at Dumbarton Oaks in Washington DC, where conversation must have turned to the subject of the half-finished *Symphony in C*, which they had commissioned from him in 1938. Ever since his arrival in America, he had been making arrangements for Vera to join him, and on 2 January 1940 she sailed from Genoa on the *SS Rex*. Stravinsky was at the quayside to meet her when she arrived on 13 January, though since she had lost her voice on the voyage she had to get one of the other passengers to shout her greeting for her. (The institutional puritanism of 1940s America also meant that he wasn't allowed to visit her in her berth.) The newly reunited couple went to Pittsburgh, where Stravinsky was conducting, and from there he travelled to Cambridge while she spent a month with a friend in Charleston. At the beginning of March, they met up again in Boston. On the 9th they were married in Bedford, Massachusetts.

When Stravinsky's lectures ended in May, they set off on honeymoon by boat from New York, but hated their destination, Galveston, Texas. Changing plan, they headed for Houston, but hated that too. By the end of the month they were in California, where they had decided to make their home, and rented a house at 124 South Swall Drive, Beverly Hills.

In July and August, the couple travelled to Mexico, where Stravinsky conducted his own and others' works, including Tchaikovsky's *Second Symphony*, in Mexico City. On 8 August, they re-entered the United States as Russian Non-preference Quota Immigrants and immediately applied for naturalisation. A few days later, back in Beverly Hills, Stravinsky finally completed the *Symphony in C*.

The *Symphony* is one of Stravinsky's major works, and his first essay in anything like conventional symphonic form since his student *Symphony in E Flat*. As might be expected, however, the conventionality lies skin-deep, limited, effectively, to the quasi-classical sequence of the movements. The opening Moderato all breve pays lip-service to sonata form but obeys dynamics altogether different from those traditionally associated with it. One of its most striking features is its metrical regularity: very unusually for Stravinsky, it is written in 2/2 time throughout. The reposeful slow movement, composed in the aftermath of the family tragedies at Sancellemoz, could be cited as evidence, were any needed, that, with Stravinsky as with any composer of genius, one should expect no neat correlation between art and life. The *Symphony* straddles the second great divide of the composer's career. But without knowing that the first two movements were written in Europe and the last two the best part of a year later in America, one would hardly hear the fault line Stravinsky himself claimed to detect in the work, the unity of which runs deeper than such formal devices as the return of the first movement's main theme at the end of the finale. Stravinsky gave the first performance of the *Symphony* in Chicago on 7 November.

Chronologically the first work of his American period, the *Symphony* really belongs to Stravinsky's European years. In October 1940, however, he finished his first composition to be written entirely on American soil – a smouldering little *Tango* for solo piano, which was first performed under Benny Goodman the following year in an authorised instrumental version by Felix Guenther. (Stravinsky's own orchestration dates from 1953.)

Stravinsky had described his works in the first years after Russia became closed to him in 1914 as 'samplings, experiments, amalgamations'. Much the same can be said of the works of his first years in the United States. Once again, he was an exile in an unfamiliar environment; once again, cultural life was feeling the pinch of war, as were Stravinsky's finances. But in much of the music he wrote during the Second World War, the imperative is far more overtly commercial than was the case during the First. A work such as the *Tango*, for example, was a frank potboiler, intended to form the basis for spin-offs such as a dance band version and a popular song. Others began life as film scores which never came to fruition. In some, such as the *Four Norwegian Moods* of 1942, the imprint of Stravinsky is in parts so light as to be scarcely perceptible to anyone hearing them without prior knowledge. Most notorious of all perhaps is the *Circus Polka*, written to be danced by circus elephants. During the 1920s and 1930s the composition of individual works may often have been interrupted by Stravinsky's commitments as a performer, but they were seldom interrupted by other *compositions*. In the early American years, on the other hand, works were routinely set aside while other commissions were accepted and completed. Ever since *The Firebird*, of course, he had cultivated the freelancer's art of getting people to commission works he had already begun. But there is a palpable difference in the music of this first American period. Not only is there a relaxation in the creative tension which had characterised Stravinsky's work up to the *Concerto for Two Solo Pianos*; it is as if he has lost his sense of musical direction – or at least is allowing it to be dictated principally by the need to earn a living. The *Symphony of Psalms* is a product of inner necessity; the fiftieth anniversary of the Boston Symphony Orchestra simply helped to crystallise it. One cannot imagine the *Circus Polka* forming in Stravinsky's mind in the hope of a future patron.

That said, his next work, the *Danses concertantes*, commissioned by the Werner Janssen Orchestra of Los Angeles, did indeed incorporate material Stravinsky had already sketched – the first notations appear with those for the final movement of the *Symphony in C*, the main theme of which is strikingly similar to that of the *pas d'action* in the *Danses*. He began work on the new composition as soon as the *Tango* was finished, but broke off time after time during the next 15 months as other opportunities presented themselves. As a result, it was January 1942 before the score was completed, and the Werner Janssen Orchestra finally premièred it the following month. Despite the title, the *Danses concertantes* was always intended for concert performance. However, Stravinsky was now taking a multiple-choice approach to his compositions and clearly had an eye to the possibility of its being danced at some stage, as indeed it was by the recently-formed Ballet Russe de Monte Carlo in New York in 1944 to choreography by Balanchine. (Balanchine was becoming a regular collaborator. In New York in January 1941, Stravinsky conducted a performance of the ballet *Balustrade* which Balanchine had made from his *Violin Concerto* and which the composer described as one of the most satisfactory visualisations of any of his works.)

That Stravinsky's finances were indeed in a parlous state is indicated by the fact that in March 1941 he took on his one and only composition pupil, Ernest Anderson, to whom he gave more than 200 lessons over the next two years. (Heretofore, apart from his informal sessions at Harvard, Stravinsky's teaching experience had been limited to classes given with Nadia Boulanger in Paris and Fontainebleau in the 1930s. There were to be no more Andersons.)

On 6 April, the Stravinskys moved into their first permanent home together and the first home of any kind the composer had owned since leaving Russia. This was 1260 North Wetherly Drive, Hollywood, where they were to live until 1964 (when they moved to another house in the same street). It was a modest single-storey house with low ceilings – Vera said it might have been designed with Stravinsky's height in mind – and panoramic views from its front terrace over the valleys of Hollywood and Beverly Hills. Light and friendly, with vasefuls of flowers reflected in numerous mirrors and rubber plants pressing against the ceilings, it was also as crowded as a small museum. Tables and shelves were lined with Russian cups, spoons, samovars, clumps of coral, paperweights; the walls were covered with icons, maps, cartoons and paintings, most of the latter either by Vera herself or the gifts of friends, including Bakst, Larionov, Goncharova and Picasso. Amazingly, the Stravinskys shared this cramped space with up to 40 caged lovebirds and a parakeet called Popka, which, apparently exempt from the strictures of Stravinsky's legendary fastidiousness, not only shared their mealtimes but would often leave a trail of droppings on the table as it did so. Stravinsky also built up a library to match his father's in imperial St Petersburg, and by the end of their tenure the house contained some 10,000 volumes, classified by language, author and subject – the 'compulsion for order' again – with art books, poetry and detective novels occupying the most shelf-space.

Stravinsky's soundproofed study was placed as far as possible from the kitchen, so that he wouldn't be put off by cooking smells, which he claimed interfered with his hearing. There he composed, as he had always done, at a muted upright piano with a plywood drawing board attached to the music stand.

The Stravinskys conducted an active social life from North Wetherly Drive. Vera shared Thomas Mann's view that 'war-time Hollywood was a more stimulating and cosmopolitan city than Paris or Munich had ever been' and described it as a 'ferment of composers, writers, scientists, artists, actors, philosophers and genuine phonies', whose lectures, exhibitions, concerts and other performances they attended – though they often read Dostoyevsky together after Hollywood parties 'to remind ourselves about human beings'. During their first

American decade, their inner circle was made up of Russian emigrés such as the choreographers George Balanchine and Adolph Bolm, the painter Eugene Berman and the actor Vladimir Sokoloff; their doctors, gardeners and domestic staff also tended to be Russian. The majority of their other friends were refugees of one nationality or another, including the pianist Artur Rubinstein, the writer Franz Werfel and his wife (Mahler's widow Alma) and the violinist Joseph Szigeti. From the 1950s, the Stravinskys' closest friends included Aldous and Maria Huxley, W H Auden, Christopher Isherwood and Gerald Heard. A roll-call of their numerous acquaintances would include many of the household names of war-time Hollywood, including such movie legends as Chaplin, Hitchcock, Dietrich and Edward G Robinson. (A conspicuous absentee was Arnold Schoenberg, who had been living in Los Angeles since 1936. It is a sad indictment of the dogmatism of twentieth-century musical life that its two most influential figures should have lived within a few miles of each other for more than a decade without making contact.) Since there was only one bedroom in the house, overnight guests had to sleep on a couch; their heights were assiduously recorded on one of the doorframes.

Interior at 1260 North Wetherly Drive: Stravinsky, Madeleine and Darius Milhaud and Nadia Boulanger (1945)

News of the war in Europe was a frequent and distressing topic of conversation for Stravinsky at this time (as well it might have been – he had, after all, left his daughter Milène an invalid in a sanatorium in France, which was by now under Nazi occupation). In May 1941, as German troops prepared to invade Russia, his only remaining brother Yury died in Leningrad, though the news didn't reach Stravinsky until the end of the year, by which time the city of his birth was already suffering the first months of its devastating two-year siege. The war impinged in more domestic ways too, especially after the attack on Pearl Harbor in December 1941: as part of the war-effort, the Stravinskys grew their own vegetables, Vera noting as a red-letter day the evening they ate borscht made from beets Stravinsky himself had cultivated; they also kept chickens for a while. (The neighbours complained about the rooster's habit of crowing at three o'clock in the morning, and one night Vera locked it in their bedroom cupboard, from which it issued in the morning like a cork out of a bottle, rushing round the room with a broom-wielding Stravinsky in pursuit!)

The chickens were not his only contribution to the patriotic cause to meet with a decidedly mixed response. Stravinsky was obliged to begin his war-time concerts with a rousing rendition of the *Star-spangled Banner*, and on 4 July 1941, acting on a suggestion by Ernest Anderson, he made his own arrangement of the piece, which he thought an improvement on the official versions. He even sent the manuscript to the First Lady, Eleanor Roosevelt, to be auctioned for war-funds, but it was returned with an apology. Worse was to follow. When he performed it in Boston, he wrote in *Memories and Commentaries*

'I stood with my back to the orchestra and conducted the audience, who were supposed to sing but didn't. Though no-one seemed to notice that my arrangement differed from the standard offering, the next day, just before the second concert, a Police Commissioner appeared in my dressing-room and informed me of a Massachusetts law forbidding any "tampering" with national property. He said that policemen had already been instructed to remove my arrangement from the music stands... I do not know if my version has been performed since.'

In November, Stravinsky had just played the piano score of the *Danses concertantes* to Vera for the first time when George Balanchine telephoned him with what must surely rank as the most surreal proposal of his career. This was for the *Circus Polka*, a short ballet piece to be danced by a troupe of elephants from Barnum & Bailey's circus to Balanchine's own choreography. In his usual businesslike way, Stravinsky established exactly what was required, accepted the commission, and by 5 February had completed the piano score. The *Circus Polka*, and its attendant ballet, was first performed in Madison Square Garden, New York, on 9 April 1942, in a wind-band version by David Raksin. The next day's *New York Times* called it 'breathtaking' and gave the following account of the 'Ballet of the Elephants', which shows, if nothing else, how little headway the notion of animal (or for that matter women's) rights had made among the American public of the 1940s!

'The cast included fifty ballet girls, all in fluffy pink, and fifty dancing elephants. They came into the ring in artificial, blue-lighted dusk, first the little pink dancers, then the great beasts. The little dancers pirouetted into the three rings and the elephant herds gravely swayed and nodded with the music. In the central ring Modoc the Elephant danced with amazing grace, and in time to the tune, closing in perfect cadence with the crashing finale [a galumphing quotation from Schubert's *Marche militaire*]. In the last dance fifty elephants moved in endless chain around the great ring, trunk to tail, with the little pink ballet girls in the blue twilight behind them. The ground shook with the elephants' measured steps.'

A backstage observer noted how undignified the bull elephants looked in their ballet dresses (no mention was made of the composer's or choreographer's dignity) and how close Stravinsky's rhythms came to causing a stampede. Nonetheless, the ballet ran to an astonishing 425 performances.

As we have seen, Stravinsky's relations with the Hollywood film industry were not of the easiest, and in later years he was scathing about the whole genre of 'film music'. Despite the lesson of *Fantasia*, however, he continued to talk to various studios, and even discussed with Disney the possibility of an animated version of *Renard*. Neither this nor any of the other movie projects he discussed came to fruition, but some got far enough for him to start writing music. One such – a projected film about the Nazi invasion of Norway – resulted in his next composition after the *Circus Polka*. His music was rejected by the studio concerned, but recycled as a concert suite, *Four Norwegian Moods*, the un-Stravinskyan title deriving from the composer's less than idiomatic English at this stage of his career (the French *Quatre pièces à la norvégienne* is both more accurate and more characteristic). The work is closely based on melodies from a collection of Norwegian folk music Vera Stravinsky had picked up in a second-hand bookshop in Los Angeles. Unlikely as it may seem, *Four Norwegian Moods* provoked the fury of younger French composers, including Pierre Boulez, when it was performed as part of a festival of Stravinsky's music in Paris after the liberation. Stravinsky himself compared these 'howling manifestations' to those at the Théâtre des Champs-Elysées more than 30 years earlier,

and it is an index of his gift for both self-reinvention and controversy that one can scarcely imagine two more different catalysts for Parisian outrage than *Four Norwegian Moods* and *The Rite of Spring*.

Four Norwegian Moods was completed in August 1942. One evening the previous month, Stravinsky had turned in for the night when he heard footsteps on the stairs up to the front door, and, as Robert Craft tells the story (in *Stravinsky in Pictures and Documents*), opened it to find on the doorstep a tall, shy man who greeted him in Russian and apologised for calling so late. The visitor had brought with him a jar of natural honey, which he'd been told was a favourite food of the composer, together with an invitation to dinner. He was Sergei Rachmaninov. It is further evidence of the cosmopolitan nature of Hollywood society in the 1940s that Stravinsky should have met his older contemporary here rather than in their native Russia or, for that matter, in Switzerland, where they had also been neighbours for a while. Rachmaninov promised that music would not be discussed over dinner (his and Stravinsky's aesthetic values were poles apart) and the two men and their wives exchanged hospitalities. Rachmaninov was notoriously taciturn, however – Stravinsky famously described him as 'a six-and-a-half-foot-tall scowl' – and the social tone of these evenings can be judged from the following snippet of table talk (or lack of it) in Stravinsky's reminiscences:

'Mme Rachmaninov: "What is the first thing you do when you rise in the morning?"'…

'Myself: "For fifteen minutes I do exercises taught me by a Hungarian gymnast and Kneipp Kur maniac, or, rather, I did them until I learned that the Hungarian had died very young and very suddenly, then I stand on my head, then I take a shower."

'Mme Rachmaninov: "You see, Serge, *Stravinsky* takes showers. How extraordinary. Do you still say you are afraid of them? And you heard Stravinsky say that he exercises? What do you think of that? Shame on you who will hardly take a walk."

'Rachmaninov: (Silence.)'

Rachmaninov died in March of the following year.

Stravinsky's next work also had its origins in an abortive film collaboration, this time on Orson Welles' classic 1943 adaptation of Charlotte Brontë's *Jane Eyre* (for which Aldous Huxley wrote the screenplay). Stravinsky had written the music for a hunting scene by the time he dropped out of the project. This became the second movement, 'Eclogue', of the *Ode*, an elegiacal chant in three parts commissioned by Koussevitzky in memory of his wife Natalie, who had died in 1942. The first performance of the work, conducted by Koussevitzky in October 1943, was a disaster: the trumpet player transposed his part wrongly in the final movement, playing it flat throughout; and two systems of score were copied as one, resulting in a cacophonous ending. According to Stravinsky, Koussevitzky himself didn't notice anything amiss, however, and, when the composer later corrected the score, confided that he preferred 'the original version'!

It was also in 1943 that Stravinsky discussed one of the most bizarre movie projects to come his way. In August, he attended a casting interview with Warner Brothers to play himself in a film about George Gershwin. (The part eventually went to a better-qualified candidate.) The film perpetuated the story, characteristic even if apocryphal, that when Gershwin asked Stravinsky for composition lessons, the latter's response was to ask him how much he earned.

On receiving a six-figure answer, Stravinsky reportedly replied, 'In that case, it is I who should take lessons from you'.

In January 1944, Stravinsky conducted the first performances of *Four Norwegian Moods* and his own orchestration of the *Circus Polka* at a concert in Cambridge, Massachusetts. The following month, he completed the score of the *Sonata for Two Pianos*, a kind of delayed postscript to the *Concerto for Two Solo Pianos* of 1935. In contrast to the earlier work, though, Stravinsky himself performed the *Sonata* in public only once, and then not with his regular *Concerto* partner, his son Soulima, but with Nadia Boulanger, who also gave the first performance, with Richard Johnston, in August 1944. In March of the same year, he also attended his first concert in Los Angeles' influential Evenings on the Roof series, which was to première a number of his compositions and which reminded him of the Evenings of Contemporary Music in the St Petersburg of his youth.

The four commissions Stravinsky fulfilled in 1944 neatly illustrate the variety of his musical stimuli during these early years in America. They are a mixed bag indeed. In April, he responded to a proposal from the music publisher Nathaniel Shilkret, who was putting together a composite suite based on the early chapters of the book of *Genesis*. He had lined up a number of eminent composers then resident in America, including Schoenberg (who was to write the 'Prelude'), Milhaud ('The Fall of Man'), Castelnuovo-Tedesco ('The Flood') and others (including Bartók, Hindemith and Prokofiev, all of whom subsequently dropped out). Shilkret himself contributed 'The Creation'. Stravinsky's part in all this was *Babel*, a self-contained seven-minute cantata for narrator, male chorus and orchestra, which recounts the biblical story of the building of the eponymous tower. The result is something of a hybrid, combining spoken and sung text as he had in *Persephone* and would again in *A Sermon, a Narrative and a Prayer* and *The Flood*. The brooding opening strikingly recalls the first bars of *The Firebird*, as the Lord's scattering of the people of Babel does the 'Laudate Dominum' of the *Symphony of Psalms*. Stravinsky sets the words of God in two parts, as he also would in *The Flood* 18 years afterwards, though here they are sung by tenors and basses rather than the two basses of the later work. *Babel* was Stravinsky's first setting of English words.

In the summer, he was approached by the Broadway showman Billy Rose to provide the music for a revue, *The Seven Lively Arts*, in return for a fee of $5,000. A short suite, *Scènes de ballet*, was written quickly between June and September, the closing 'Apotheosis' reflecting, Stravinsky said, something of the jubilation he felt at the liberation of Paris, news of which came through on the radio as he was composing it. The composer's friend Ingolf Dahl, his closest musical colleague at this period, arranged the music for piano page by page as it was written, and it was despatched to Rose, who seemed happy enough with it. But the orchestral version was a different matter, and after the preview performance in Philadelphia Stravinsky received a telegram reading 'Ballet great success stop... Can the Pas de Deux be orchestrated with the strings carrying the melody this is most important to insure greater success.' The composer telegraphed back: 'Satisfied great success.' Nonetheless, the music was cut ruthlessly for the show's Broadway run. Stravinsky himself called the *Scènes de ballet* 'featherweight and sugared', a description most obviously applicable to the notorious *pas de deux*, whose swelling strings upend the music into the very sentimentality it seems to be parodying.

The same summer he completed for Paul Whiteman's jazz band the catchy *Scherzo à la russe*, which he rescored for conventional symphony orchestra in May the following year. Described by Mihaud as 'very *Petrushka* 1944', this distant Hollywood echo of the ballet's 'Russian Dance' is yet another recycling of unused film music, this time for *North Star*, a propaganda piece in which Russian villagers defend themselves against the Nazi hordes.

The final commission of the year was the short *Elegy* for solo viola, composed for the violist Germain Prévost in memory of Alphonse Onnou, the founder of the Pro Arte Quartet. It was first performed in Washington DC in January 1945, and was choreographed by George Balanchine later the same year.

For the last two years, however, Stravinsky had been working on something of far greater substance than these assorted 'little masterpieces-for-money' as Robert Craft has called them. In April 1942, he had begun a work which may originally have been conceived as a concerto, but which took shape as a symphony – the *Symphony in Three Movements*. The first movement was completed in October 1942, just after the full score of the *Circus Polka*; the second in March 1943, just after the middle movement of the *Ode*. He then laid the work aside for more than two years.

As we have seen, 1944 was devoted to other commissions, concerts and lectures. Stravinsky seems also to have undergone another spiritual crisis during this year, visiting a

Dominican convent in Sinsinawa, Wisconsin, and spending a lot of time in the company of the religious philosopher Jacques Maritain, whose writings had been an influence on him ever since Lourié introduced him to them in the 1920s. In December, Stravinsky finished the first two movements of a *Mass*, which was to have an even longer gestation period than the *Symphony*, achieving its final form only in 1948, and 1945 began with a series of concerts and recordings in New York and a course of lectures in Philadelphia. In April, he made his third suite from *The Firebird*, and the following month, as the war ended in Europe, completed the orchestral version of the *Scherzo à la russe*. Only then did he return to the unfinished *Symphony*, adding the third and final movement in August, as the war in the Far East also came to a close.

The *Symphony in Three Movements* is the first major work of Stravinsky's American period, and comes as an explosion of Dionysian energy after the Apollonian restraint of the *Symphony in C*. Indeed, it is one of the composer's fiercest scores, reminiscent at times of *The Rite* in the rhythmic drive of its outer movements. The calmer central movement is in fact based on yet more undeployed film music, in this case for the apparition of the Virgin in Franz Werfel's *The Song of Bernadette* (the fulfilment of a vow Werfel had made when sheltering at Lourdes, the scene of St Bernadette's vision, during his flight to the US from Nazi-occupied France). Stravinsky later described the *Symphony* as a 'war symphony' and gave an uncharacteristically programmatic account of its relation to the world events amid which it was written. He even went so far as to claim that 'each episode in the Symphony is linked in my imagination with a concrete impression, very often cinematographic in origin, of the war', the first movement being inspired by footage of scorched-earth tactics in China and of Chinese peasants scratching for food in the fields, and the last by documentary newsreels of goose-stepping Nazi soldiers. Typically enough, though, after laying out these associations at some length in his *Dialogues*, Stravinsky abruptly repudiates the whole idea of the *Symphony* being a programmatic work at all – or indeed of its even being a symphony in any real sense ('perhaps Three Symphonic Movements would be a more exact title').

The final work of 1945 was the delightful *Ebony Concerto*, written for Woody Herman's jazz band. Stravinsky's most extended essay in jazz form, it is also one of his most enduringly popular pieces. The composer himself described it as a 'jazz *concerto grosso* with a blues slow movement', and

Woody Herman and his jazz band, for whom Stravinsky wrote his *Ebony Concerto*

glossed 'Ebony' as referring not to the clarinet, for which the concerto has a solo part, but to the supposed African origins of blues music. Stravinsky studied the Herman band's recordings while writing the work, and even employed a saxophonist to teach him fingering. A few months after the première, he recorded the work in a studio so fogged with smoke from the musicians' cigarettes that 'the atmosphere looked like Pernod clouded by water'.

The *Ebony Concerto* was completed on 1 December. In the same month, Stravinsky underwent his second and final change of nationality. A Russian in exile since 1914, he had been a naturalised Frenchman for the past 11 years. On 28 December 1945, he officially ceased to be an alien in his new adopted country and became a citizen of the United States of America.

Chapter 8

The American citizen (1946-1951)

One immediate effect of Stravinsky's newly acquired citizenship was that it enabled him to safeguard the copyright of his earlier works in the US by producing revised versions of them. These were published by the British firm Boosey and Hawkes, who took over all the works previously published by the Edition Russe de Musique. Under this arrangement, over the next seven years Stravinsky made new versions of, among other things, *Petrushka*, the *Symphonies of Wind Instruments*, *Apollo*, *Oedipus Rex*, the *Symphony of Psalms*, the *Capriccio*, the *Concerto for Piano and Wind Instruments*, *Persephone*, *The Fairy's Kiss* and the *Octet*. Some of these revisions were substantial, as in the case of *Petrushka* and the *Symphonies*; others were limited to refinements and the correction of errors.

A less tangible effect of naturalisation seems to have been a change in Stravinsky's personality. Obviously, American citizenship didn't transform him overnight. But many people who had known him in Europe bore witness to the fact that, almost from the moment he settled in the United States, he began to seem more relaxed and approachable. The camera tells the same story. Before the 1940s it is so rare to find a photograph of Stravinsky smiling that the grins of so many later pictures come as something of a shock. The fastidiousness in dress remains – age did not ruffle Stravinsky's much-remarked dandyism – but the aristocratic monocle, the haughtily inflexible bearing, have been replaced by a new informality. At 64, Stravinsky was as open to new influences and ideas as ever, and the relatively unbuttoned ways of California clearly rubbed off on him – albeit reversibly, as Robert Craft, who entered Stravinsky's life in 1948, was to discover when he accompanied the composer to Europe in 1951. The most important influence of all, though, remained his wife Vera, and one senses a new order of happiness in the couple as they began to build a domestic life for themselves free from the burden of guilt and tragedy which had darkened their final years in France.

One of Stravinsky's first public engagements as an American citizen was the première of the *Symphony in Three Movements*, which he conducted in New York on 24 January 1946. The *Ebony Concerto* received its first performance two months later at Carnegie Hall, with Walter Hendl conducting the Woody Herman Band. (Stravinsky himself couldn't be there: his ever-punishing concert schedule took him to Baltimore, Cambridge, Boston, Havana, Dallas and San Francisco in the early months of the year.) The *Concerto* was broadcast a few days later, after which the Woody Herman Band took it on tour. Not until August did Stravinsky conduct the work himself.

In the same month, he completed a new concerto, the *Concerto in D* for string orchestra, often known as the 'Basle', since it was written for the twentieth anniversary of the Basle Kammerorchester. Ironically enough, given that it was Stravinsky's first composition as a US citizen, the concerto was also his first European commission for more than a decade. Indeed, it was the only one to come his way from the Old World between 1933, when he started work on *Persephone*, and 1955, when he wrote the *Canticum Sacrum*. Like the 'Dumbarton Oaks' *Concerto*, with which it is often bracketed, the 'Basle' is in three movements, the first and last of which have some of the forward drive, but none of the aggression, of the *Symphony in Three Movements*. The second is a waltz-like 'Arioso' and is the only movement in which the writing recalls that of *Apollo*, Stravinsky's only other work for string orchestra. The *Concerto* was given its first performance by its dedicatees, the Basle Kammerorchester and their conductor Paul Sacher, in Basle on 27 January 1947.

By this time, Stravinsky was already at work on another major commission. Lincoln Kirstein of the Ballet Society of New York had approached him early in the year with a proposal for a ballet on the Orpheus legend to be choreographed by Balanchine. *Orpheus* was begun in October 1946 and finished a year later, composer and choreographer working closely together throughout in a way more characteristic of the Diaghilev years than of Stravinsky's recent works for the musical theatre.

Their scenario divided the action into three scenes and 12 episodes. The ballet opens with desolate descending scales on the harp (representing the Orphic lyre and meant to sound 'dry and choked') as Orpheus, 'motionless, with his back to the audience', laments the loss of Eurydice; the first scene continues with the Angel of Death leading him to Hades. The second scene begins with an ominously quiet dance of the Furies; Orpheus then charms the underworld with his lyre in an interrupted *air de danse*, which the lost souls implore him to continue and at the end of which the Furies blindfold him and reunite him with Eurydice. The lovers dance a *pas de deux* – the ballet's longest number and its emotional centre of gravity – but Orpheus is unable to restrain himself from looking at Eurydice once more and, as the orchestra falls silent for a single bar, tears the blindfold from his eyes. Eurydice immediately dies for the second time, and the Bacchantes set upon Orpheus, tearing him limb from limb – the only moment in the score when Stravinsky unleashes the full orchestra. The third and final scene enacts Orpheus' apotheosis at the hands of Apollo and begins with the return of the slow descending harp scales of the opening. The ensuing fugue of two horns is suddenly cut off and the harp is heard rehearsing what Stravinsky seems to have conceived as a kind of accompaniment to the enduring song of Orpheus; the fugue then resumes as if nothing had happened.

The score of *Orpheus* breathes an air of mournful restraint unlike anything else in Stravinsky. The music remains soft throughout, rising to fortissimo only once, briefly, at the moment of Orpheus' dismemberment. It is as if one were observing the action through a veil of mist, an effect realised in the transparent curtain which descended during the 'Interludes' in Isamu Noguchi's original staging. *Orpheus* received its first performance, under Stravinsky's baton, on 28 April 1948 in New York and was a tremendous success (even if, as the composer later observed, Orpheus' protruding mask made him look like a baseball catcher!). It was to be the last of his ballets on an overtly classical theme.

'Because so much of *Orpheus* is mimed song,' the composer wrote in *Themes and Conclusions*, 'it seemed inevitable to me that my next work would be an opera.' Indeed, ever since he had arrived in the United States, Stravinsky had been thinking of writing an opera in English, and in May 1947 a visit to a Hogarth exhibition at the Art Institute in Chicago had given him his theme. He had been fascinated by the engravings of Hogarth's series the 'Rake's Progress', which tells the story of a young man's decline into libertinism, madness and death, and the idea of using them as the basis for a series of operatic scenes was already fully formed by the time he finished *Orpheus* in October. Before *The Rake's Progress* could be written, however, there was a long-standing work-in-progress to complete. This was the *Mass*, the 'Kyrie' and 'Gloria' of which had been written as long ago as December 1944.

The Tavern Scene from Hogarth's 'Rake's Progress' (1735)

Like the *a capella* sacred choruses of 1926, 1932 and 1934, the *Mass* was a direct expression of Stravinsky's religious faith. Unlike them, however, it was intended for use not in his own Russian Orthodox Church, but as part of the Roman Catholic service. The composer explained this somewhat uncharacteristic ecumenicalism in purely musical terms: instruments were forbidden in Russian Orthodox services, and he couldn't stand unaccompanied singing except in 'the most harmonically primitive music'. He also famously claimed to have been provoked into writing a 'real' mass by some Mozart masses – 'rococo-operatic sweets of sin' – he found in a second-hand music shop in Los Angeles in the early 1940s. Whatever the inspiration, the *Mass*, which is sparely scored for winds only, has an extraordinary quality of timelessness, most evident perhaps in the rapt interweavings of high vocal and instrumental lines in the 'Gloria'. The 'Credo', the density of whose text has been a perennial challenge to composers, is here largely chanted, its intensity heightened by the low dynamics. At a dinner with Evelyn Waugh in February 1949, Stravinsky drew a striking analogy: 'One composes a march to help men march; and it is the same way with my Credo: I hope to provide some help with the text. The Credo is long. There is much to believe.' Like the *Symphony of Psalms*, this is music of great devotional power, more suited (despite its first performance at the Teatro della Scala, Milan) to the church than to the concert platform, and Stravinsky himself expressed disappointment that it did not find a more regular place in the liturgy.

The *Mass* was completed in March 1948. At the end of the previous year, Stravinsky had his first meeting with the man who was to provide him, in *The Rake's Progress*, with one of the finest of twentieth-century opera librettos. Wystan Hugh Auden was recommended as a librettist by Stravinsky's Hollywood neighbour and close friend of these years, the novelist and critic Aldous Huxley. In September 1947, Stravinsky wrote to his new publisher, Ralph Hawkes, asking him to contact Auden on his behalf, and in November the poet visited the composer in Hollywood, where he underwent the North Wetherly Drive ritual of being measured for the guest couch (it had to be extended with a chair and pillows to support his feet). Auden stayed for a week, during which time the two men worked out a detailed scenario for the opera. They also attended, in a local church hall, a two-piano performance of the opera in which, in a curious syntactical inversion, Stravinsky described *The Rake* as being 'deeply involved', Mozart's *Così fan tutte*. (If Mozart had been the negative inspiration for the *Mass*, his is the tutelary spirit of *The Rake*. Not only was *Così* almost the only opera Stravinsky would listen to when writing it; there are also many correspondences between *The Rake* and Mozart's own tale of a libertine's progress, *Don Giovanni*.)

Composer and librettist presented a striking contrast: Stravinsky fastidious, ordered, driven; Auden dishevelled, ambling, domestically haphazard. But Auden was as completely professional a poet as Stravinsky was a composer, and their collaboration on *The Rake's Progress* was to be one of the most rewarding of the latter's life. From the first, the correspondence between the two men reveals a true meeting of minds, and a deep respect for each other's craftsmanship. 'It is the librettist's job to satisfy the composer, not the other way round,' Auden wrote – a sentiment which must have been music to Stravinsky's ears after his disastrous non-collaboration with Gide on *Persephone*. Always ready to amend to the composer's specifications, he would adjust his lines to the requirements of the music and supply new material in complex metres by return of post. There were moments of tension, of course, notably when Auden subcontracted parts of the libretto to his long-time companion Chester Kallman

without informing Stravinsky in advance. But overall it was, in the composer's words 'a collaboration in the highest sense'. 'He *was* inspired,' Stravinsky wrote, 'and he inspired me.' He regarded the Auden-Kallman libretto, the first two acts of which were delivered by the end of January 1948, the third two months later, as a match for those paradigms of the genre, Da Ponte's librettos for Mozart. Auden, for his part, developed an abiding affection for Stravinsky: 'Too often in my life' he wrote, 'I have met persons whom I revered but found myself unable to love; less often, I have met persons whom I loved but found myself unable to revere. I have met Igor Stravinsky and find myself able to do both: what a joy that is!'

The Rake's Progress is Stravinsky's only full-length opera, both *The Nightingale* and the one-act *Mavra* being miniatures of the form. It was also his first extended setting of English words (*Babel* being his only previous essay in this line). As such, it demonstrates the huge advance he had made in mastering the language of his adopted country – his own fourth language and one which he could manage at best stumblingly when he first arrived. At two and a half hours, *The Rake* is by far the longest of Stravinsky's works, and from March 1948, when he finished the *Mass*, and April 1951, when he completed the opera's 'Epilogue', he devoted himself to it to the exclusion of any other composition. This sustained labour was all the more remarkable for the fact that, unusually among Stravinsky's major works, *The Rake* was not commissioned. He was therefore devoting three years of his creative life – the writing took him precisely as long as he estimated it would at the outset – to a project which provided no guarantee either of income or of performance.

The Rake's Progress is in three acts and follows Hogarth's series only in broad outline. In the Stravinsky-Auden-Kallman version, the action takes place in the space of a single year. Act One opens on a spring afternoon in the burgeoning garden of Truelove's country cottage. The anti-hero, Tom Rakewell, and Truelove's daughter Anne sing of their love, and Tom, of whom Truelove is suspicious, wishes he had money. Immediately, the sinister servant-figure Nick Shadow appears and informs Rakewell that he has inherited a fortune from an uncle and should go to London to sort out the details. The lovers bid each other farewell, swearing constancy, as Shadow addresses the audience with the phrase 'The progress of a Rake begins'. The scene shifts to summer, London and Mother Goose's brothel, where, after singing a beautiful cavatina to love, Tom allows himself to be drawn into the general revelry. Back in the country, in autumn, Anne laments her lover's silence and determines, in a vigorous cabaletto, to join him in the city.

At the beginning of Act Two Tom is weary of vice ('Vary the song') and makes a second wish – to be happy. Again, Shadow appears on cue and proposes that he prove his superiority to the urgings of his lower nature by marrying Baba the Turk, the bearded lady from St Giles' Fair. Anne arrives in London on the day of the wedding, and learns the truth when she encounters Tom and Baba outside his house. By winter the marriage has broken down, and in the final scene of the Act, after a crockery-smashing quarrel, Tom renounces Baba to devote himself to improving mankind. Quick to exploit this third wish, Shadow wheels on a fraudulent machine for converting stones into bread, and while Tom rapturously serenades its possibilities for the universal good, Shadow exhorts him to seek financial backing for this 'excellent device'.

By the start of Act Three, spring has come round again and Tom has been bankrupted by the venture. All his possessions, including his wife Baba, who has remained in exactly the same chair since he pushed her there at the end of the previous Act, are auctioned off. The same night Rakewell and Shadow meet in a ghostly churchyard, where Shadow reveals himself as the devil and demands payment for his services in the form of Tom's soul. He challenges Tom to a game of cards, but when Tom wins three times, Shadow admits defeat and, in terrible rage, curses him instead with insanity. Shadow sinks into the grave he had prepared for Tom, the stage goes dark, and when the lights come up again, the grave is covered with a green mound on which Tom, his reason gone, sits threading grass in his hair and singing pathetically that he is Adonis, the lover of Venus. The final scene, like Hogarth's, takes place in Bedlam, where Tom is visited by Anne, whom he believes to be his Venus. He asks her forgiveness and she sings him a poignant lullaby, after which her father Truelove fetches her away and Tom, bereft, lies down and dies. At this point, the music abruptly changes character and, in an 'Epilogue' which, like the graveyard scene, owes a transparent debt to *Don Giovanni*, the characters doff their wigs and, addressing the audience directly, point the deliberately reductive moral:

'For idle hands
And hearts and minds
The Devil finds
A work to do.
A work, dear Sir, fair madam,
For you and you.'

Although Stravinsky had made no provision for performance of the work when he began it – and despite the fact that he refused to play it for any non-musician while he was working on it – by 1951 various opera houses were vying for the right to stage the première. In February of that year, he concluded an agreement with the Venice Biennale to conduct the first performance at the Teatro la Fenice as part of the fourteenth

International Festival of Contemporary Music in September. His fee for the one night was $20,000. In August, accompanied by Vera and Robert Craft, Stravinsky returned to Europe for the first time since he left France 12 years earlier. He contracted pneumonia on the voyage, but two weeks later was well enough to conduct rehearsals at La Scala, Milan, which was providing the opera company. His arrival was greeted with the sort of welcome normally reserved for international film stars. Auden and Kallman joined him in Milan, but having neglected to book a hotel in advance, were reduced to renting rooms by the hour in a local brothel! In the first week of September, the company was translated to Venice, where the world première of *The Rake's Progress* took place on the 11th.

Rehearsing *The Rake's Progress* at La Scala, Milan, in 1951

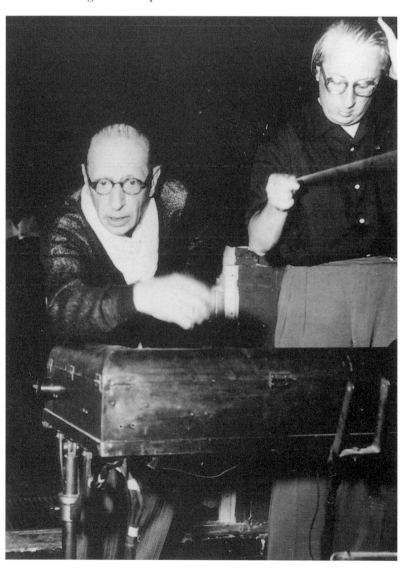

The sense of occasion was palpable. For hours before the performance, the press lined the surrounding streets for a glimpse of the great and good, who arrived by gondola and motor launch at the canal-side entrance to the theatre. Amid the jewellery and evening dress, tricorned soldiers manned the doors and bouquets of roses adorned the boxes. Stravinsky's arrival in the orchestra pit was greeted with fervent applause. The performance was by all accounts somewhat under-rehearsed, but there were few left unmoved by the music, and when it ended, at one o'clock in the morning, the composer was given an ecstatic ovation. The Stravinsky party retired to the Taverna La Fenice, where the celebrations went on until dawn.

Stravinsky liked to describe *The Rake* as a conventional opera, and in its succession of arias, ensembles and dry and accompanied recitative (the former employing harpsichord), it draws openly on eighteenth-century models. The music, though, is Stravinskyan to the core and demonstrates a gift for melodic invention to which he had rarely if ever given such rein before. Such moments as Rakewell's cavatina 'Love, too frequently betrayed', or his final meeting with Anne in Bedlam, are among the most profoundly moving passages in the music of the twentieth century. But *The Rake's Progress* marks a term in Stravinsky's output. If his previous opera, *Mavra*, stood at the beginning of his 'neo-classical' period, *The Rake* stands at its close. Perhaps its sheer self-sufficiency left him few avenues to explore without a radical change of direction. Perhaps too he was shocked to find that, for many of the younger generation of European musicians, for whom Schoenberg represented the future, it cast him still more irredeemably as a reactionary. Whatever the truth, Stravinsky himself was to speak of the period after its production as representing his 'second crisis' as a composer – a crisis no less profound, if shorter in duration, than that occasioned by the loss of Russia more than 30 years earlier. It was a period from which he would emerge, his language once more redefined, into an Indian summer of creativity for which there are few parallels in the history of music.

Crucial to the process which would result in that remarkable final flowering of Stravinsky's protean talent was the entry into his life, during the writing of *The Rake's Progress*, of the young Robert Craft. Craft, a 23-year-old conductor with a rapidly growing reputation as an interpreter of contemporary music, wrote to Stravinsky in the summer of 1947, asking if he could borrow the (then unobtainable) score of the *Symphonies of Wind Instruments*. He was presenting a series of concerts with the Chamber Art Society in New York and wanted to include the *Symphonies* in one of his programmes. Stravinsky, who had coincidentally just completed his revised version of the work, wrote back offering to conduct it himself; he was even, uncharacteristically enough, prepared to waive his fee. On 31 March 1948, the two men met, together with Auden who was delivering the last Act of *The Rake*, at the Raleigh Hotel in Washington DC – an encounter vividly described in the first diary entry of Craft's *Stravinsky: Chronicle of a Friendship*.

Stravinsky and Robert Craft during rehearsals for *The Rake's Progress* at La Scala, Milan, in 1951

At the beginning of the following year, Stravinsky asked Craft to spend the summer at North Wetherly Drive, sorting and cataloguing his manuscripts, which had recently arrived from Paris. Craft agreed and in June 1949 installed himself on the Stravinskys' famous guest couch before moving a few blocks away to a house the composer had rented for his son Soulima and family. During these summer months, Craft's role swiftly expanded beyond the cataloguing of the crated manuscripts to helping Stravinsky answer the piles of letters which arrived for him every day, advising him on the rhythmic values of the English language in Auden's libretto for *The Rake*, and accompanying the Stravinskys on their hectic social round. By the time he returned to New York in September he had become their constant companion, and the remarkable chemistry between himself and the composer, which has since been the subject of so much puzzled analysis, not least by Craft himself, had firmly established itself. Given Stravinsky's capacity for falling out with his closest musical associates, such intimacy might well have proved a poisoned chalice. In the event, it was the beginning of an extraordinarily fertile relationship which would endure for the remaining 23 years of Stravinsky's life.

The formative musical experiences of Craft's life dated to 1940, when he had heard both *The Rite of Spring* and Schoenberg's *Pierrot lunaire*. The music acted on him with the force of revelation, and he proceeded to sink himself in study of the two composers' work, developing a depth of specialist knowledge in which he was to have few equals. What's more, in his devotion to *both* Stravinsky and Schoenberg, he straddled the artificial divide erected by, among others, his predecessor as Stravinsky's musical right-hand man, Arthur Lourié. It was a balancing act which continued into the period when he first became a part of the Stravinskys' family circle. He was one of very few visitors, for example, to be equally welcome at North Wetherly Drive and Schoenberg's Los Angeles home, and even if mention of each was taboo in the other he remained a kind of bridge between them. Not until he had finished *The Rake's Progress*, though, did Stravinsky take steps to make the crossing himself, and by then, in the very nature of the catalyst, it was too late for a personal reconciliation.

1950 and 1951 had seen the deaths of a number of the composer's friends and former associates, including Nijinsky, Adolph Bolm and Koussevitzky, and at the end of 1950 Stravinsky himself was worried that he might die before finishing *The Rake*. Then, on 14 July 1951, Craft brought to North Wetherly Drive the news that Schoenberg had died the

The constant companion:
Robert Craft with Stravinsky in
1950

previous night. In stark contrast to the apparent indifference with which he had greeted the passing of Nijinsky and Koussevitzky, Schoenberg's death affected Stravinsky far more deeply than anyone could have foreseen. He immediately dictated a telegram of condolence to the composer's widow, and it was only when Vera persuaded him that it might be misinterpreted as ironic that he gave up the idea of attending the funeral (and this in a man who had to be persuaded *to* attend his own mother's). At the same time Schoenberg's death seems to have liberated him from whatever sense of rivalry may, up until then, have prevented his making more than the most cursory acquaintance with the older composer's work. From then on, however, under Craft's evangelical guidance, he began to explore the music not only of Schoenberg, but also of those other titans of the Second Viennese School, Alban Berg and, most influentially of all for his future development, Anton Webern, of whose complete works Craft was soon to embark on a ground-breaking series of recordings.

In his seventieth year, with the toil and triumph of *The Rake's Progress* behind him, and at an age when many men might have been tempted to rest on their creative laurels, Stravinsky stood on the threshold of his final, and in many ways his most controversial, period of self-renewal.

Chapter 9

The second crisis (1952-1957)

On 8 March 1952, on an afternoon of lightly falling snow, the Stravinskys and Robert Craft were driving home from lunch in a cowboy grill in Palmdale when Stravinsky, suddenly on the verge of tears, declared that he feared he could no longer compose. It was a deeply uncharacteristic access of self-doubt in the man widely regarded as the world's greatest living composer, and a disturbing revelation of the depth of the creative crisis into which the completion of *The Rake's Progress* and his new exposure to the music of the Viennese serialists had plunged him.

Throughout January and February, Stravinsky had been attending Craft's rehearsals of Schoenberg's *Suite* (Septet) Op. 29 for a concert which also included Webern's *Quartet* Op. 22. These sessions were often followed by hours of questioning and discussion, as Stravinsky sought to understand from Craft the disciplines behind the music. 'After 40 years of dismissing Schoenberg as "experimental," "theoeretical," "*démodé*,"' Craft confided to his diary, 'he is suffering the shock of recognition that Schoenberg's music is richer in substance than his own.'

Whatever the truth of the musical assessment, the effect of the shock can be felt in the composition on which Stravinsky had just resumed work in earnest. Apart from a therapeutic post-Palmdale rearrangement for 12 instruments of his 1920 *Concertino* for string quartet, the *Cantata*, a setting of anonymous medieval English lyrics begun in July 1951, was his first work to be completed after *The Rake*. A few days before the Palmdale crisis he had finished the movement in which his music first engages with serial techniques, the long and severely beautiful 'Ricercar' for tenor, cello, flutes and oboes 'Tomorrow shall be my dancing day'. The mysteriously resonant verses, a first-person allegory of the life of Christ, are set to a series of canons on a note-row which, while not consisting of the strictly Schoenbergian 12 notes, is subjected to the full gamut of serial procedures: it appears in retrograde (played back-to-front), inversion (upside-down) and retrograde inversion (back-to-front and upside-down). For many years Stravinsky had built his music from small cells, often of limited compass, and had increasingly stiffened his textures with counterpoint. The *Cantata*, however, takes that process a stage further. The result is one of his most haunting works, in which the two 'Ricercars' and a setting of the exquisite lyric 'Westron wind' are punctuated by verses for female chorus from the funereal 'Lyke-wake dirge' – the latter the first of several coincidences with the work of his young English contemporary Benjamin Britten, who had set the same words, much more starkly, in his 1943 *Serenade* Op. 31 for tenor, horn and strings. Stravinsky presented Craft with the manuscript score of the passage 'And through the glass window shines the sun', inscribed 'To Bob whom I love'.

While Stravinsky's creative life was in turmoil, his outward career remained as busy as ever. He spent May in Paris, where he met Albert Camus and conducted *Oedipus Rex*, with Cocteau as the Speaker, at the Théâtre des Champs-Elysées, the scene of the *Rite of Spring* riot four decades earlier. The second performance, on a double-bill with Schoenberg's *Erwartung*, prompted a mini-riot of its own when the concert was interrupted by hecklers hostile to Cocteau; Stravinsky, in the audience on this occasion, left the theatre. While he was in Paris, an interviewer asked him about serialism, and he revealed his still equivocal attitude in the famous reply: 'Personally I find quite enough to do with seven notes of the scale. Nevertheless, the serial composers are the only ones with a discipline that I respect. Whatever else serial music may be, it is certainly pure music. Only, the serialists are prisoners of the figure twelve, while I feel greater freedom with the figure seven.'

At the beginning of June he accepted an invitation to celebrate his seventieth birthday in Holland, where he was characteristically unawed by his lavish reception as guest of honour. Craft describes the occasion vividly in his diary:

'Queen Juliana and her ministers, ambassadors, generals: I have never seen so much pomp and gold galloon, so many epaulettes, medals, and swords... At intermission... the Queen sends for I.S., bids him sit next to her, declares her admiration for his "works," and is not only taken aback but also struck dumb by his response: "And which of my works do you admire, Your majesty?" The programs ends with his

String Concerto, in which nearly everything, including the tempo relationships in the first movement, is wrong. When the conductor, Van Otterloo, presented to I.S. afterward, asks how he liked the performance, I.S. snaps: "Do you want a conventional answer or the truth?" Van O. manfully opts for the latter, which is "Horrible!"'

Stravinsky's actual birthday, by contrast, was spent fuming about the service in a downbeat diner on the banks of Lake Superior.

The *Cantata* was finished on 21 July 1952, hours after North Wetherly Drive was rocked by a miniature earthquake. The very next day, Stravinsky began work on his *Septet*, during the composition of which he again regularly attended Craft's rehearsals, this time for a series of Schoenberg memorial concerts in the autumn. He also gave the premières of the *Cantata* and the revised *Concertino* at Royce Hall in November, and went on to perform both works in New York, where he celebrated Boxing Day at a bibulous dinner with Auden and finished the *Septet* on 21 January 1953.

The *Septet* was written for the Research Library and Collection at Dumbarton Oaks, and is scored for clarinet, horn, bassoon, piano, violin, viola and cello. A work the texture of which is governed by counterpoint to a greater extent than any of his previous compositions, it represents a further step in the direction of serialism. As Paul Griffiths has pointed out, the first movement, which inhabits a similar sound-world to that of Stravinsky's earlier Dumbarton Oaks commission, the *Concerto in E flat*, is the last of his original compositions to have a key signature. Both the second movement, a grave 'Passacaglia', and the concluding fugal 'Gigue' (a title shared with the finale of Schoenberg's septet *Suite*), treat their closely related themes as note-rows. The music betrays nothing of the crisis of confidence in which it was forged, its unity and spirit belying the transitional place it occupies in Stravinsky's oeuvre.

During his three months on the East Coast, Stravinsky attended the New York première of *The Rake* at the Met in February and recorded the opera, with Craft's assistance ('Robert is my ears' he told the players) at the Columbia studio at the beginning of March. On 5 March, he had lunch with Salvador and Gala Dali, Dali approaching the outrageousness of his image only in his assertion that 'the houses of the future will be soft and hairy'. The same day saw the deaths of both Stalin and Prokofiev, the latter upsetting Vera but apparently leaving Stravinsky cold. Six days later, the Stravinskys returned to Los Angeles, but at the end of the month the composer was on his travels once again, this time to Havana, Caracas (where he said the sounds of the jungle at night focused around F sharp) and Boston. In his absence, the ice was finally broken between the Schoenberg and Stravinsky households with an exchange of dinner invitations by Vera and Schoenberg's widow.

'As soon as I saw him, I knew that the only thing to do was to love him': Dylan Thomas, whose death in 1953 deprived Stravinsky of a keenly anticipated collaboration

While Stravinsky was in Boston, he met Dylan Thomas to discuss an opera collaboration which was destined to remain one of the great might-have-beens of twentieth-century music. Vera Stravinsky had been impressed by one of the poet's legendary public readings in Urbana in 1950, and when Boston University offered to commission a new opera from Stravinsky, Craft suggested Thomas as librettist. The poet arrived in the state of advanced seediness which characterised his American tours, and Stravinsky, himself ill in bed, instantly succumbed to his vulnerable charm. 'As soon as I saw him,' he later recalled, 'I knew that the only thing to do was to love him.' Gouty, chain-smoking and blotchy from too much alcohol, Thomas proposed as a subject 'the rediscovery of love and language in what might be left of the world after the bomb'. Stravinsky, apparently untroubled by the poet's formidable reputation for

160

unreliability, was greatly excited by the prospect, and Thomas sealed their rapport with a moving impromptu recital of Yeats' long ballad 'The Wild Old Wicked Man'. The Stravinskys invited him to stay with them during his next visit to the States, and even built an extension to North Wetherly Drive to accommodate him. On 9 November, however, waiting for news of his arrival time, they received instead a cable from a London newspaper asking Stravinsky for a comment on his death, which had occurred that afternoon in a New York hospital. He was 39. Stravinsky went to his study and wept. The new guest room was henceforth always to be known as the Dylan Thomas Room.

In July, Stravinsky underwent surgery to remove his prostate. The operation seems to have sapped some of the animal energy which had astonished observers for more than half a century, but nonetheless left him enough for a schedule of international engagements which, barely slackening well into his eighties, would have tested the reserves of a man half his age. 1953 was the only year between 1950 and 1967 that the Stravinskys didn't go to Europe, and it seems probable that they would have moved to Italy permanently had it not been for Stravinsky's health.

During September and October, Stravinsky continued his exploration of English word-setting in the *Three Songs from William Shakespeare* for mezzo-soprano, flute, clarinet and viola. A further step along the road to full serial technique, the three settings – 'Musick to heare' (Sonnet VIII), 'Full Fadom five' (from *The Tempest*) and 'When Dasies pied' (from *Love's Labour's Lost*) – were also his first group of songs since the *Four Russian Songs* of 1919 (two of which he was shortly to arrange for voice, flute, harp and guitar). The refinement of scoring recalls the *Three Japanese Lyrics* and the *Pribaoutki*, as do such mimetic touches as the 'Ding-Dong' tolling of the bell in the second song and the delicately avian coda to the third.

October saw the premières of the *Praeludium* for jazz ensemble and the instrumental version of the *Tango*, which Robert Craft gave at one of the Evenings on the Roof concerts (soon to metamorphose into the Monday Evening Concerts). Then on 24 January, the *Septet* received its first performance at Dumbarton Oaks. In between, Stravinsky sketched the opening fanfare of a new ballet, later to be called *Agon*, which had been commissioned by the New York City Ballet in August, but which he now laid aside to write a deeply felt memorial tribute to Dylan Thomas.

Pierre Monteux (1875-1964), the first conductor of *The Rite of Spring*, for whose eightieth birthday Stravinsky wrote the *Greeting Prelude*. By Milein Cosman

In Memoriam Dylan Thomas is the first of several funerary works composed to the memory of Stravinsky's friends and contemporaries during the final phase of his creative life. At its heart lies an anguished setting for tenor and string quartet of Thomas' famous poem on the death of his father, 'Do not go gentle into that good night'. This is framed by a desolate 'Prelude' and 'Postlude' for string quartet and four trombones, the latter added once Stravinsky knew the forces available for the concert at which Craft proposed to perform the work. As its subtitle 'Dirge-Canons and Song' suggests, this is an austerely contrapuntal work, and since its material derives entirely from a single five-note set, devotees of Schoenberg were not slow to claim its composer as a fully-fledged convert to the cause of serialism.

In Memoriam was completed in June 1954, on Stravinsky's return from a two-and-a-half-month European tour during which he conducted in Rome, Turin, Lugano, London and Lisbon (and would have conducted in Geneva had he not confused his medicine bottles and gargled with formaldehyde on the eve of the concert!). After rehearsals at North Wetherly Drive, Robert Craft premièred *In Memoriam* at a Monday Evening Concert in September, by which time Stravinsky had resumed work on *Agon*. In the last quarter of the year, he directed staged performances of an earlier ballet, *Petrushka*, in Chicago, San Francisco and Los Angeles. Then in December he received another commission, this time for a sacred work – the *Canticum Sacrum* – to be performed in St Mark's Basilica, Venice, as part of the 1956 Biennale, and *Agon*, now half-completed, went back into cold storage.

1955 began with concerts in Portland, Salem, Birmingham and Atlanta. In February, Stravinsky wrote the tiny *Greeting Prelude*, a kind of 'singing telegram' for the eightieth birthday of his old friend Pierre Monteux, the first conductor of *The Rite of Spring*. The *Greeting* is a good-natured serial squib on the theme 'Happy Birthday to you', which Stravinsky had first heard a few years earlier when, to his irritation, the orchestra he was rehearsing in Tchaikovsky's *Second Symphony* struck up with it to congratulate one of the players. In contrast to Stravinsky's earlier brush with the copyright laws with the popular song he'd used in *Petrushka*, the composer of 'Happy Birthday' did not press for royalties.

From March to May, Stravinsky was away from home on another European tour, starting in Lisbon (where he learnt he'd been awarded the Sibelius Medal) and continuing to Spain, Italy, Germany, Switzerland, Austria and Denmark. In Austria, he visited Mittersill to lay flowers on the grave of Anton Webern, whom he would soon describe as 'a perpetual Pentecost for all who believe in music'.

In June, he returned to Hollywood and for once stayed put for six months at a stretch. He used the time to write the whole of the *Canticum Sacrum*, finishing it, with the best part of a year in hand, on 21 November 1955. At less than 20 minutes, however, the *Canticum* was a little short for the proposed Biennale programme, and in December, during a visit to New York, he began work on a filler, an arrangement of Bach's Chorale-Variations on *Vom Himmel hoch* using more or less the same forces as the *Canticum*. This was finished on 27 March 1956 and dedicated to Robert Craft, who found the inscribed manuscript on his plate when he came to lunch that day. Craft gave the variations their first performance at the Ojai Festival in California in May.

In the summer of 1956, Stravinsky sailed for Europe on the *SS Vulcania*. From Naples, he made a pilgrimage to the castle of Gesualdo, the sixteenth-century Prince as famous for ordering the murder of his wife as for the advanced harmonic language of his madrigals. Stravinsky had become fascinated by Gesualdo's work after hearing it in Craft's rehearsals a couple of years earlier. Indeed, he had originally intended to include a Gesualdo arrangement in the *Canticum Sacrum* programme, but the Venetian authorities forbade the performance in St Mark's of works by a Neapolitan.

Stravinsky continued to Sicily and Greece, sightseeing in Athens and Istanbul before finally arriving in Venice on 30 July. There he was ferried to the palace of the Patriarch, soon to become Pope John XXIII, to receive formal permission for the concert to take place in St Mark's. The Stravinsky party then went to San Michele to lay flowers on Diaghilev's grave, but the composer, ever superstitious, refused even to set foot on the island (15 years later it would become his own last resting place). The remaining days before the première were spent in a round of rehearsals, visits and sightseeing.

On 13 September 1956, in the presence of the Patriarch and 3,000 guests of honour, Stravinsky conducted the first performance of the *Canticum Sacrum ad Honorem Sancti Marci Nominis* in the candlelit Basilica of St Mark. Interest in the occasion was so intense that the music was relayed by loudspeakers to the waiting crowds in the Piazza outside, who applauded Stravinsky as he left the cathedral. Nonetheless, the new work was greeted by incomprehension in many quarters, the music critic of *Time* savagely despatching it as 'Murder in the Cathedral'. Scored for tenor and baritone soloists, chorus and orchestra (including, for the first and only time in Stravinsky's output, the organ), the *Canticum* begins with a brief introductory 'Dedication' ('To the City of Venice, in praise of its patron saint, the Blessed Mark, Apostle') sung by the soloists. The text of the rest of the work is drawn from the Vulgate. The five movements, in which some have seen a reflection of the quintuplex ground-plan of St Mark's itself, are cyclical in form, the last being a near-perfect retrograde version of the first. At the centre of the work lies the long third movement, itself in tripartite form, celebrating the Christian virtues of love, hope and faith (in that order); the heart of the *Canticum* is thus a hymn to hope. The second movement, the tenor solo 'Surge, aquilo' ('Awake, O North wind' from the *Song of Songs*), is Stravinsky's first serial work to use a 12-note set, and is balanced by the fourth movement, which is also predominantly for a soloist (the baritone). The *Canticum Sacrum* is pre-eminently music for St Mark's. Not only does it pay conspicuous homage to the Venetian tradition of Gabrieli and Monteverdi, whose works were performed in the same space; it is also specifically scored for the resonant acoustic of the Basilica, as witness the frequent pauses to let echoes subside.

Stravinsky's own resources of hope and faith would soon be sorely tested. Immediately after the première, he embarked on a concert tour, which took him to the still war-devastated city of Berlin. Here, on 2 October, while he was conducting the first movement of his *Symphony in C*, he blacked out. After a long pause, he was able to continue with the rest of the programme, but the following day his speech was slurred and the right side of his body felt numb. He insisted on continuing with his gruelling schedule, however, and flew to Munich. Here his refusal to see a doctor was overruled and a mild stroke diagnosed, with the warning that a massive one might follow within 24 hours. Finally, more than a week after his blackout, Stravinsky was admitted to hospital, where he remained until 17 November. For the rest of his life he would work under the threat of death or paralysis from another stroke brought on by what was believed to be the blood disorder polycythemia. His medical régime involved weekly blood-tests and monthly treatment by bloodletting or radioactive phosphorus, and his health became a matter of international public interest. Nonetheless, his creative and performing schedule remained dauntingly full, and he refused point-blank to give up smoking or alcohol. Within 12 days of his discharge from hospital he was not only conducting the *Canticum Sacrum* in Rome, but celebrating in a restaurant afterwards until three o'clock in the morning.

In London in December, he met T S Eliot for the first time, and despite a somewhat inhibited tea at the Savoy the two men went on to become friends. Nine years later, Eliot would be the subject of another of Stravinsky's funerary tributes, the *Introitus*. He also sat next to Ralph Vaughan Williams at a concert in St Martin's-in-the-Fields, but the two composers failed to recognise or speak to one another. At the end of the month he returned to New York where, in January 1957, with his old Diaghilev colleague Massine in the control room, he made a recording of *Persephone*. Back in Los Angeles in the spring, he heard Pierre Boulez' *Le Marteau sans maître* conducted by the composer, with whom Craft was now in close contact. Then, on 26 April, the fiftieth anniversary of the first performance of his *Symphony in E Flat*, he finally completed the much-interrupted *Agon*.

Agon – the title of which means 'contest' – is the last of Stravinsky's 'white' ballets, and the last transitional work of his pre-serial period. Completing it must have presented him with a similar challenge to that of *The Nightingale* when he returned to it after the rapid musical evolution of

The Firebird, *Petrushka* and *The Rite of Spring*. It was almost two and a half years since he had put his first thoughts on paper, and his musical language had meanwhile undergone another radical transformation. Only six years separate *Agon* from *The Rake's Progress*, but in its synthesis of serial and non-serial techniques and its unprecedented variety of instrumental colour, *Agon* belongs to a different musical world. At the same time, it is as characteristically Stravinskyan as anything he had written since *The Firebird*. During the First World War, C F Ramuz had identified an 'act of possession' as Stravinsky's characteristic response to anything that engaged his interest – the composer himself described it as 'a rare form of kleptomania' – and his use of serialism, in *Agon* as in the more strictly serial works which were to follow, is as much an appropriation as his use of Pergolesi in *Pulcinella*. As Otto Klemperer was to observe, 'Stravinsky's switch... from tonal music to the twelve-tone row changes only the style of his music. His face remains the same.' Indeed, since Stravinsky continued to compose 'vertically' and acknowledged that the intervals of his series were 'attracted by tonality', it is questionable whether he ever became an 'atonal' composer in the strict sense of the word at all.

Agon stands as an exhilarating climax to Stravinsky's lifetime's work as a dance composer, and since its first concert performance by Robert Craft in June 1957 it has established itself as one of his most popular works. Although the music employs serial techniques very freely, the whole conception of *Agon* is informed by the number 12. It is written for 12 dancers, for example, and has 12 movements, arranged into four groups of three, separated by a 'Prelude' and two 'Interludes' of closely related music. The movements of the second and third groups are the ones most obviously influenced by the manual of seventeenth-century dance music Stravinsky had to hand throughout the composition. The work is full of breathtakingly original sonorities, perhaps the most unearthly of which occurs in the 'Gailliard' [*sic*], where harp and mandolin recall the steps of a courtly dance in the acoustical space between low strings and high flute and string harmonics; the effect is as if one were listening to the music from an immeasurable distance. Rather as the 'Fisherman's Song' returns at the end of *The Nightingale* to link the earliest music with the later, here, but with far greater success, the serial idiom of the final 'Four Trios' folds seamlessly into a repetition of the opening fanfare, creating a marvellous sense of homecoming.

Most astonishing of all perhaps is the fact that music of such youthful zest and vigour should come from the pen of a sick man a few months short of his seventy-fifth birthday. Nor did his pace let up now. In the two days after the *Agon* première he recorded it and the *Canticum Sacrum*. Then, after a holiday in Santa Fe, which would be a regular resort in future summers, he was off on his travels again. First port of call was England for a festival of his music at Dartington Hall in Devon – a visit which afforded the unlikely vignettes of Stravinsky savouring a glass of stout in a pub in Totnes and attending Agatha Christie's long-running West-End murder mystery *The Mousetrap*! Next stop was Paris, where he was entertained by Pierre Boulez. In Venice from the end of August, he lunched with the one-time surrealist artist Giorgio de Chirico and dined with the American composer Elliott Carter. In the next few weeks he travelled to Munich, where he had dinner with Hindemith, and Baden-Baden to rehearse *Agon*, performances of which he then gave in Paris, Donaueschingen and Rome.

In November he returned to New York, where the ballet première of *Agon* took place on the 27th. But Stravinsky didn't attend. By now his energies were so fully absorbed in a new work that he had already left for Los Angeles to continue it at home. The composition was to be one of his greatest sacred works, and with it begins the final phase of his creative life.

Chapter 10

The final flowering (1957-1966)

It was on 29 August 1957, in the incongruous setting of a basement nightclub in Venice, that Stravinsky sat down at the piano to start work on *Threni*.

In the recording studio: Stravinsky and Robert Craft at Abbey Road in 1958

The work was the result of a commission by the North German Radio Orchestra of Hamburg for the 1958 Venice Biennale. The negotiations had been somewhat bumpy, with Stravinsky, for whom God and Mammon were by no means incompatible masters, characteristically insisting on $1,000 more than the $10,000 he was offered, and equally characteristically blowing at least that amount on a dinner for friends, including the very people he'd just been negotiating with, when he got them to agree to it! Health and engagements notwithstanding, work proceeded apace, and the score was finished on 21 March 1958. It is the first in which Stravinsky derived all his musical material from the orders of a single 12-note series, and thus ushers in the characteristic idiom of his final period as a composer.

'Your twelve-tone rows will cause an uproar in the musical world and will keep analysts busy,' Erwin Stein had predicted when he heard *Canticum Sacrum* in 1955. Certainly, few bodies of work have generated as dense an output of analytical literature as Stravinsky's from *Threni* onwards. The composer himself complained that his late music was more discussed than performed, and there is no doubt that, for all its immediacy of texture, colour and effect, it presents a greater challenge to the listener than the works of his so-called 'Russian' or 'neo-classical' periods. As ever with Stravinsky's restless self-reinvention, however, the continuities are as striking as the change. Even the notoriously austere *Threni* conveys first and foremost an atmosphere of devotional intensity which belongs unmistakably to the same emotional world as the *Symphony of Psalms* and the *Mass*, and has its origins in the same love of ritual which informs *Zvezdoliki* and *The Wedding*, not to mention such instrumental works as the *Symphonies of Wind Instruments*. Indeed, it is as if the serial technique has itself become part of the ritual. As Stravinsky once remarked, 'the manner of saying and the thing said are, for me, the same'.

Threni: id est Lamentationes Jeremiae Prophetae is a setting of the lamentations of the prophet Jeremiah for soloists, chorus and orchestra. (*Threni* – 'threnodies' or 'songs of mourning' – is the title of the Elegies of the Jeremiad in the Vulgate, from which the text is drawn.) Although the work is in three movements, the massive central movement is divided into three parts: 'Querimonia' (complaint), 'Sensus spei'(sense of hope) and 'Solacium' (repayment or comfort). The structure is therefore similar to the five-movement framework of *Canticum Sacrum*, with hope once more at its core – a similarity enhanced by the short declamatory introduction ('Incipio'), again sung here by two soloists. The severe contrapuntalism of the score, most striking perhaps in the progression of canons, each with one more voice than the last, in the four verses of the 'Querimonia', is punctuated by choral markers in the form of the Hebrew letters (Aleph, Beth, etc.) which introduce each section of the text like stations of a spiritual journey. Another striking feature of the score is the use of unpitched chanting in the framing movements – a distinctive new development in Stravinsky's music and one which will recur in the sacred works of his final years. The large orchestra includes sarrusophone and flügelhorn (the latter supposedly inspired by Shorty Rogers' jazz trumpet), but its full forces are never deployed. Instead, small groups of instruments are used in shifting combinations, the music coming finally to rest in a short stoic coda for four horns.

Threni was first performed at the Scuola di San Rocco in Venice on 23 September 1958, with Stravinsky conducting. The new work polarised opinion, proving that at 76 Stravinsky had lost none of his talent for putting the cat among the pigeons. For those who had followed his banner as the leader of the anti-Schoenberg tendency, it was seen as an unforgivable act of desertion. For others, it was evidence of his continuing ability to infuse new life into his work. One outspoken critic of Stravinsky's music between the wars, for example, wrote breathlessly that 'the grandeur of this score, its formal unity, austerity, beauty, its rejection of all compromise, all "effects", all sensual seduction, all personal sentiment, gives proof once more, after your Mass and cantata to St. Mark, of the continuing youthfulness of your genius.' The première was dedicated to the memory of Alessandro Piovesan, the director of the Venice Biennale, whose death in February had greatly saddened the composer.

Immediately after the performance, Stravinsky took the work on tour to Switzerland and Germany. In November, he conducted *Oedipus Rex* at the Vienna State Opera, lunched with the sculptor Alberto Giacometti in Paris, and in Rome was invited to the Vatican by Pope John XXIII, whom he'd met as Patriarch of Venice and who asked for his autograph after the audience. In London in December, he renewed his acquaintance with T S Eliot and met Graham Greene at a dinner party with Stephen Spender before returning to New York by sea before Christmas.

1959 was a significant year for Stravinsky in a number of respects. For one thing, it began a new phase in his public life. If his travel schedule had seemed highly paced up till now, from 1959 it went into top gear. The next four years, leading up to his eightieth birthday in 1962, were to see concert tours of Japan, Latin America, Australasia, South Africa, Israel and, climactically, Russia, as well as his usual round of engagements throughout Europe and the United States.

1959 was also important for the publication of *Conversations with Igor Stravinsky*, the first of a series of books based on conversations between the composer and Robert Craft. These publications, which also include letters, media interviews and, in their earlier editions, excerpts from Craft's compellingly readable diary, have been the subject of some controversy; in particular, there has always been debate about the respective contributions of their two originators. Certainly, as Craft was the first to admit, the Stravinsky of these replies has a powerful command of English not readily apparent from recordings or broadcasts. At the same time, the language and manner is convincingly idiosyncratic, and the dialogue form, in which the composer typically treats

Stravinsky at the podium: two views by Milein Cosman

each question as the springboard for a freely associative series of memories, opinions and analyses of his work, is clearly far more congenial to him than the constraints of his stiltedly conventional *Autobiography*. There is never any doubt that one is in the presence of a singularly forceful personality, however much that personality may be a dual construct, and the five books into which the series was later rationalised remain the indispensable primary resource for Stravinsky's views of his life and work.

Most important of all, in the *Movements* for piano and orchestra 1959 saw another startling evolutionary jump in Stravinsky's appropriation of serial technique to the distinctive musical language of his final years.

The year began with the US première of *Threni*, conducted by Robert Craft at the Town Hall, New York. Then in March the Stravinskys were guests at an archetypal Hollywood ball in the Beverly Hilton, at which Vera danced with Vincent Price and Harpo Marx joined them at their table. At the end of the month, the Stravinsky party flew to Tokyo via Honolulu, Manila and Hong Kong for the start of a five-week tour of Japan, where the composer was received with great warmth. He conducted in Tokyo and Osaka – by now his concerts were generally rehearsed by Craft, who would divide the programme with him – and visited the sights, taking away a lasting impression of the 'rhythmical orderliness' of Kabuki theatre and an interest in Japanese music which he fed with records on his return to the US. For much of the time, the Stravinskys were accompanied by one of their closest friends of these years, Nicholas Nabokov (the cousin of the novelist), who had been instrumental in prompting the trip.

The composer conducting a performance of *Oedipus Rex* for the BBC in 1959. Jean Cocteau is sitting at the far left

Stravinsky returned to Hollywood in May, but was at home for only a few days before flying off again, this time to Copenhagen to receive the first Sonning Prize and conduct the *Octet* and the *Firebird* suite in the presence of the Danish King and Queen. During the short interim at North Wetherly Drive, he composed the brief but haunting *Epitaphium* for flute, clarinet and harp in memory of his friend Prince Max Egon zu Fürstenberg, the patron of the Donaueschingen Festival, which he had attended as the Prince's guest for the last two years. (The *Epitaphium* was the first of two funerary tributes composed in 1959. The second, the *Double Canon* for string quartet, has the greater tragic intensity, despite being dedicated to the memory of a man Stravinsky had never actually met, the painter Raoul Dufy. Stravinsky's non-musical reactions to the deaths of contemporaries seem to have been comparably unpredictable.)

In August, Stravinsky completed a composition he had been working on since the summer of 1958 – the *Movements* for piano and orchestra. After *Threni*, which is far the longest of his late serial works, the tendency of Stravinsky's musical thought is decisively towards compression, and nowhere is this trend more arrestingly evident than in *Movements*. Perhaps the most concentrated score he ever wrote, this miniature piano concerto lasts barely 10 minutes. In its crystalline complexity, however, it bears out Stravinsky's own description of his late work as containing very much more music for its time span than his pre-serial compositions. Here there are five movements, each linked to the next by a short coda which establishes the new tempo. While technically *Movements* deploys similar serial procedures to those used in *Threni*, stylistically it could hardly be more different. Indeed, Stephen Walsh has described it as marking the most abrupt stylistic change in the whole of Stravinsky's output. The composer himself called it 'the most advanced music from the point of view of construction' that he had ever composed and regarded it as the 'turn-of-the-corner' in his later work. Certainly, it perplexed the audience at its first performance, which took place in New York in January 1960, with Stravinsky at the podium and the work's dedicatee Magrit Weber at the keyboard.

Shortly after completing *Movements*, Stravinsky had his first discussions about a new commission, *The Flood*, a proposed dance-dramatisation of the Noah story for CBS Television. He also travelled to Britain, where he dined with Eliot in London, spent a few days in Edinburgh and was bowled over by Laurence Olivier's *Coriolanus* at Stratford. The rest of September and early October 1959 were spent in Venice, where he wrote the *Double Canon*. After a further round of concerts and sightseeing in Italy, he returned to London for two weeks, and thence to New York at the end of the year.

1960 was the putative four-hundredth anniversary of the birth of Carlo Gesualdo di Venosa, whose music, as we have seen, Stravinsky had been studying for some time. The previous year he had arranged and completed the *Tres Sacrae Cantiones*, three of Gesualdo's incomplete sacred motets. Now, in March 1960, he finished the *Monumentum pro Gesualdo di Venosa*, a recomposition for instruments of three of the Neapolitan composer's madrigals.

The central event of the year, though, was a five-week concert tour of Latin America, which kicked off with a celebrity reception in Mexico City at the beginning of August. From there Stravinsky travelled to Colombia and Peru, where he was once again greeted more like a Hollywood film star than a Hollywood composer, his rapturous reception at a concert in Lima contrasting starkly with the boos and catcalls which marked the arrival of the country's President! Further ports of call included Santiago, where Vera heard an eye-witness describe her father's funeral in the city 25 years earlier; Buenos Aires, where Stravinsky met Jorge Luis Borges and was awarded the Order of Maya; and Rio de Janeiro. He arrived back in New York at the beginning of September, but later the same month travelled to Venice to direct the first performance of the *Monumentum pro Gesualdo* in the Doge's Palace (the inundation of the city at this time supposedly providing him with the title for *The Flood*). The *Monumentum* also formed the basis for a Balanchine ballet in New York later the same year.

Stravinsky in the recording studio at Maida Vale, London in October 1961

Back in Los Angeles in January 1961, Stravinsky continued his mammoth series of Columbia recordings with the complete *Firebird* – the first time he'd conducted the work in its entirety for more than 40 years. He also finished writing a new cantata for alto and tenor soloists, speaker, chorus and orchestra, the unwieldily titled *A Sermon, a Narrative and a Prayer*. Oddly, considering that Stravinsky had recently forsworn the uneasy mixture of spoken and sung text he'd employed in *Persephone*, *A Sermon, a Narrative and a Prayer* reverts to just such a mixture, with arguably less integrated effect. As the title suggests, the work is in three movements, the 'Sermon' taking its text from St Paul's Epistles, the 'Narrative' (in which much of the text is spoken over the music) from the account of the stoning of St Stephen in the Acts of the Apostles. The concluding 'Prayer' is drawn from the dramatist and poet Thomas Dekker (1570-1632) and is the section which comes closest to sustaining the devotional power of *Threni* or the *Canticum Sacrum*. *A Sermon, a Narrative and a Prayer* was commissioned by Paul Sacher of the Basel Kammerorchester, for whom Stravinsky had written his *Concerto in D* 15 years earlier. Its true prototype, though, is the 1953 cantata *Babel*, another experimental setting of a biblical text in English often felt to lack the musical and dramatic coherence of Stravinsky's most successful sacred works.

As in previous years, the composer spent the summer of 1961 in Santa Fe. In September, he set off on another international tour, this one lasting two and a half months and taking in Europe, Egypt and Australasia. The first leg included Helsinki, where he visited Sibelius' widow, and Stockholm, where he met the director Ingmar Bergman, whose sympathetic staging of *The Rake's Progress* he greatly admired. From Scandinavia he travelled to Germany, touring Berlin, only weeks after the building of the Wall, in the car of the city's mayor (and later West German Chancellor) Willy Brandt. Other stops on the itinerary were Yugoslavia, Switzerland and England, where he had dinner with Eliot in London, lunch with Isaiah Berlin in Oxford and tea with E M Forster in Cambridge; he also conducted *Persephone* at the Royal Festival Hall.

From London, the Stravinsky party flew to Cairo at the end of October for a few days' intensive sightseeing before embarking on the Australasian leg of the tour. Here too Stravinsky was accorded the kind of welcome which was just coming to be associated with pop stars. A group of students with 'We Dig Ig' banners greeted him at Wellington airport, and he was whisked off onto the New Zealand cocktail circuit, where, as Robert Craft recorded in his diary, he practised the gentle art of diplomatic irony:

'Large N.Z. lady to I.S.: "Frankly, Mr. Stravinsky, I like *Firebird* best of all your works." I.S.: "And what a charming hat you have."... Wife of high N.Z. dignitary to I.S.: "Do you like architecture, Mr. Stravinsky?" I.S.: "Let me think about it."'

In Sydney, he met the novelist Patrick White, and told the *Melbourne Sun* (his reserves of diplomacy now apparently running low): 'I am a composer who does what he thinks, and if people don't feel my music they can go to hell.' The return journey to Los Angeles at the beginning of December included a stop-over in Tahiti. Once again, he was at home for no more than 10 days before setting off again, now to Mexico for yet more sightseeing and concert engagements. Somewhere amid this whirl of socialising and music-making he still managed to find time to compose. His work on *The Flood* was nearing completion, and on 2 January 1962 he finished *Anthem*, a short serial setting for unaccompanied chorus of Part IV of T S Eliot's *Little Gidding* ('The dove descending breaks the air').

Vera and Igor Stravinsky with the Kennedys at the White House in January 1962

1962 was the year of Stravinsky's eightieth birthday, an event marked by celebrations of his life and music throughout the world. On 18 January, he, Vera and Robert Craft were invited to the White House for dinner with President and Mrs Kennedy – the first time, according to Craft, that an American President had honoured a creative artist in this way. The presidential limousine collected them from their hotel and after navigating the security apparatus and a scrum of paparazzi they were ushered into the presence of the first family. Over dinner, Vera told President Kennedy about the uproar which had greeted the first performance of *The Rite of Spring*, and he laughed aloud, referring to the incident later in his short speech of tribute to the composer. When, after dinner, the ladies withdrew, Stravinsky made to accompany them before being redirected to the menfolk and his seat on the President's right hand; when asked how he was feeling, he replied 'Quite drunk, thank you, Mr President'. 'Nice kids,' was his laconic assessment of his hosts in the car on the way home. Vera appears simply to have been relieved that he hadn't asked the President to reduce his tax bill!

In March, Stravinsky completed his biblical music-drama for television, *The Flood*, and Robert Craft recorded it in the composer's presence a couple of weeks later. The text, compiled by Craft principally from the York and Chester cycles of medieval mystery plays, overlaps in part with that of Benjamin Britten's 1957 treatment of the Noah story, *Noye's Fludde*; unlike Britten's work, however, *The Flood* also covers the Creation and the Fall of Lucifer and of Man. Like *A Sermon, a Narrative and a Prayer*, it mixes spoken text (here for the 'terrestrial' characters) with singing (for the 'celestial' ones). In *The Flood*, however, the modes of delivery are even more heterogeneous – narrated speech, spoken dialogue in character, solo and choral singing, even a square-dance caller – and the piece as a whole is often felt to be correspondingly uneven. Although it is the longest of Stravinsky's serial works after *Threni*, the characteristic compression of his later language tends to create the impression of a succession of short episodes, a tendency confirmed by the requirements of television as Stravinsky saw them. 'Visually' he wrote in *Dialogues*

'[television] offers every advantage over stage opera, but the saving of musical time interests me more than anything visual. This new musical economy was the one specific of the medium guiding my conception of *The Flood*. Because the succession of visualisations can be instantaneous, the composer may dispense with the afflatus of overtures, connecting episodes, curtain music.'

However, the effect of this economy tends in practice to be a certain short-windedness, with some episodes, such as Lucifer's fall from heaven or the temptation of Eve, so short in relation to their dramatic content as to appear perfunctory. It is also the reason why the pantomimic and the portentous seem more often to collide than to fuse. Most consistently effective perhaps are the two purely instrumental sections, the 'Building of the Ark', which recalls the bright fragmented textures of *Movements*, and 'The Flood' itself, the latter a rare (and eerie) example of extended mimesis in Stravinsky's music, though the composer insisted that the object of the imitation was not the flood itself but 'a time experience of something that is terrible and that lasts'. Stravinsky described his work on *The Flood* as that of 'a theatre composer doing a theatre job', and his characteristic openness to the possibilities of his new medium expressed itself in several highly telegenic ideas for the staging, which he elaborated in intensive working sessions with Balanchine in Hollywood. It did not, however, extend to his actually watching the broadcast – an unfocussed collage of drama, documentary and shampoo commercials – since by June when it went out in the US he was again away on tour.

In May, after giving concerts in Seattle and Toronto, Stravinsky had gone to Paris, where he had lunch with the expatriate Irish playwright Samuel Beckett. A couple of days later, he flew to Johannesburg at the beginning of a two-and-half-week tour of South Africa, where he gave concerts in Johannesburg, Springs (conducting an all-white orchestra before an all-black audience) and Pretoria. In June, he was in Rome and, for his eightieth birthday itself, Hamburg, where he conducted *Apollo* at the Staatsoper on a New York City Ballet programme which also included *Agon* and *Orpheus*. Back in the States in August, he made the first sketches for his next work, the 'sacred ballad' *Abraham and Isaac*, and at the end of the month flew to Israel, where the work was formally commissioned by the Israel Festival Committee and where he received his most tumultuous welcome to date. The most moving event of his week there was the gift of a history of the Jewish community of his beloved Ustilug by descendants of some of the town's inhabitants. He also met the President – invitations from heads of state being by now an occupational hazard of Stravinsky's VIP status – and toured the sights of the Holy Land.

The climax of his eightieth birthday year, though, was his return, after almost half a century's exile, to the Russia of his birth. An invitation from the Union of Soviet Composers had been received in 1961, but much political heart-searching had delayed its acceptance. On 21 September 1962, however, Stravinsky, Vera and Craft flew to Moscow at the beginning of a three-week visit to the USSR, which was to have a profound impact on the composer. Even if it was not a rehabilitation – Stravinsky's music remained rare on Soviet concert programmes afterwards as before – it was at least, after years of mutual suspicion and abuse, a rapprochement. More important for both Stravinskys, it was a homecoming. Craft recorded in his diary that he had never known the composer so moved by any experience, and he soon found Stravinsky reverting to a Russian persona he hardly recognised. He would toast composers about whose work he had always been scathing, and praise, without apparent irony, menus and facilities which would have sent him into a rage anywhere else. He even told a meeting in Moscow of Soviet composers, including Khachaturian and Shostakovich :

'I regret that circumstances separated me from my fatherland, that I did not give birth to my works here and, above all, that I was not here to help the new Soviet Union create its own music. I did not leave Russia of my own will, even though I disliked much in my Russia and in Russia generally. Yet the right to criticise Russia is mine, because Russia is mine and because I love it, and I do not give any foreigner that right.'

On 26 September, he gave a concert in the Tchaikovsky Hall, at the end of which, recalled to the stage by wave after wave of applause, he raised his hands to silence the audience and said simply 'You see a very happy man.'

The highlight of the trip was a visit to Leningrad – the St Petersburg of his childhood. Here he was met on the airport tarmac by a small but remarkable welcoming party, including 'a pale elderly gentleman wearing a hearing aid' who greeted him and began to weep. It was Vladimir Rimsky-Korsakov, the son of Stravinsky's old teacher, with whom he had sailed down the Volga in the memorable summer of 1903. Stravinsky initially failed to recognise him, for the touching reason that Vladimir addressed him as 'Igor Fyodorovich' instead of the familiar 'Ghima' of their student years. Also present were relatives of Stravinsky's co-librettist on *The Nightingale*, Stepan Mitusov; a daughter of the poet Balmont, two of whose lyrics Stravinsky had set in 1911; and one of Diaghilev's nephews. From Leningrad, Stravinsky visited his birthplace, Oranienbaum, now called Lomonosov. He also returned to the scenes of his

St Petersburg childhood, finding a bust of Lenin on the spot in the Mariinsky Theatre where he had glimpsed Tchaikovsky, and visiting the apartment block on the Krukov Canal where he had spent his formative years. Seeing the family front door for the first time in 50 years, he evinced no emotion only because, as he confided to Craft, he didn't dare to let himself. On 8 October, he conducted a concert at the Philharmonic Hall for which people had been queuing in relays for months. The farewell committee for the return train to Moscow was largely the same as the one which had welcomed him a few days earlier. Craft's incomparable diary entry reads: 'As we pull out of the station, a Diaghilev, a Tolstoy, a Rimsky-Korsakov, and a Balmont run alongside for a moment, like another era trying to catch up.'

The return of the native: Stravinsky acknowledges the applause of the audience (and Tikhon Khrennikov, Secretary of the Union of Soviet Composers) after a concert in the Grand Hall of The Moscow Conservatoire in October 1962

Back in Moscow on the last day of his trip, Stravinsky was invited to the Kremlin to meet President Khrushchev, who talked with zeal of his political reforms and whom Stravinsky afterwards likened to 'a composer showing you the score on which he is working, and of which he is very proud'. It is a remarkable testament not only to Stravinsky's personal standing, but also to the universality of his art, that in a single year – and that the tensest of the entire Cold War, the year of the Cuban Missile Crisis – he should thus have been the guest of both the President of the United States and the President of the Soviet Union.

Four years of creative life remained to Stravinsky after he returned from Russia to Hollywood in October 1962. While there was nothing to match the drama of the Russian visit, they remained years of strenuous travel, concert-giving, recordings and composition. In the final weeks of 1962 alone, at the end of a year in which he had already criss-crossed the globe to Europe, South Africa, Israel and the Soviet Union, with return trips to the US in between, he gave further concerts in Rome and Caracas and flew to Toronto to record *Zvezdoliki*, the *Four Studies* for orchestra, *Babel*, the *Scherzo fantastique* and the *Symphony in C* – and all this while continuing to work on the sacred ballad *Abraham and Isaac*.

Stravinsky had been fascinated by the possibility of setting Hebrew verse ever since he had been introduced to it by Isaiah Berlin in Oxford in 1961. In *Abraham and Isaac* – another coincidence of text with Britten – the 19 Hebrew verses of the familiar biblical story are set for a single baritone-narrator and chamber orchestra. One of Stravinsky's most powerfully original achievements, it can also seem one of the most forbidding of his late serial works, and it certainly demands repeated listening to make its full impact. Behind its textural austerity, however, lies both a love of the language – the seventh Stravinsky had set – and what he described as a 'strong extra-musical motivation', his 'gratitude and admiration for the people of Israel, to whom the score is dedicated'. He made the commission fee over to the fund for the restoration of the Massada, the ancient fortress often regarded as symbolic of the Jewish right to self-determination.

Abraham and Isaac was completed in March 1963, almost a year and a half before its first performance. In April, after further recording sessions in Toronto, Stravinsky set out on another European tour, which included Hamburg (for the first staged performance of *The Flood*, conducted by Craft), Budapest, Zagreb, Paris and London, where he attended the

Albert Hall for a fiftieth anniversary performance of *The Rite of Spring* under its original conductor, Pierre Monteux. During his stay in England, he also lunched with the art historian Kenneth Clark at his spectacular Kentish home Saltwood Castle, and visited the reclusive poet-artist David Jones in his Harrow bedsit. Further stops included Dublin, Stockholm and Milan.

Part of the summer was spent at Santa Fe, where he arranged Sibelius' *Canzonetta* Op. 62a by way of thanks for another recent award, the Wihuri-Sibelius Prize. He then travelled to Brazil, where he gave concerts in Rio and attended a sinister midnight *macumba* ceremony in the hills above the town. He was back in Europe at the end of the year for concerts in Rome and Sicily, where he also paid a visit to the widow of Tomasi di Lampedusa, the author of *The Leopard*. It was thus in a hotel in Catania that he received the shattering news of the assassination of John Kennedy on 22 November; together with Vera and Craft, he spent most of the night glued to the radio for further bulletins. Two days later, he heard that Aldous Huxley, one of his closest Hollywood friends, had also died on 22 November. By the beginning of 1964, Stravinsky was talking about writing an elegy in memory of Kennedy, and by March had received a specially written lyric from W H Auden, the four-verse *haiku* chain 'When a just man dies'. The *Elegy for J.F.K.* is set for medium voice and three clarinets and is a touching tribute to the man whose loss he felt both personally and as an American citizen. The work was given its first performance by Robert Craft at a Monday Evening Concert five days after it was completed.

The novelist Aldous Huxley (1894-1963), whom Stravinsky memorialised in the *Variations* for orchestra

Aldous Huxley was memorialised in Stravinsky's only other work of 1964 (apart from a 30-second *Fanfare for a New Theatre* composed for the opening of the New York State Theatre in New York), the *Variations* for orchestra. Subtitled 'Aldous Huxley in Memoriam', the *Variations* had been started some months before the death of their eventual dedicatee and, unlike Stravinsky's other memorial tributes of his final period, are far from funereal in tone. Indeed, in its inventiveness, wit and kaleidoscopic variety of instrumental colour, this last of all Stravinsky's orchestral works serves as a fitting summation of his life as what Debussy once called 'the most wonderful orchestral technician of our time'.

The *Variations* were completed on 28 October 1964. In June, Stravinsky had travelled to England to make his celebrated recording of *The Rake's Progress*, and in August to Israel for the first performance of *Abraham and Isaac*, returning to New York at the end of the month to find the streets outside his hotel crowded with fans of The Beatles, who were staying next door. In September, before embarking on another European tour, during which he conducted performances of *Renard* and *Capriccio* in Berlin, the Stravinskys moved house after 23 years at 1260 North Wetherly Drive. Their new home was in the same street – number 1218, the house, until her death in 1959, of their old friend the Baroness Catherine d'Erlanger, a one-time backer of Diaghilev – but it was much better adapted to Stravinsky's decreasing mobility. It also had more space than the old one, and the couple set about extending it still further, adding bathrooms, a guest room and a swimming pool, and converting existing rooms into a library and a studio. It is indicative of the changes age and sickness had wrought in Stravinsky, however, that he found the move disorientating and never really settled in the new house.

Scarcely a month went by now without the deaths of friends and colleagues. Cocteau, Hindemith and Poulenc had died in 1964, and at the beginning of 1965 news reached Stravinsky of the death of T S Eliot. Ten days later, on 14 January, he began *Introitus* (T S Eliot in Memoriam), a setting of the 'Introitus' from the Latin Requiem Mass for tenors, basses, harp, piano, two timpani, two tam-tams, solo viola and double-bass. The work was finished a month later and exudes a brooding solemnity which is wholly distinctive in the composer's output. At Stravinsky's last meeting with Eliot, just over a year earlier, the head waiter of the New York restaurant at which they were eating was heard to remark 'There you see together the greatest living composer and the greatest living poet.' As a tribute from the one to the memory of the other, *Introitus* is a deeply moving work and one which, even at this late stage in Stravinsky's composing career, points forward to new sonorities, new possibilities. The month after it was completed, he began the work for which it is in effect a preparation, the *Requiem Canticles*. It was to be his last major composition.

In the early summer of 1965, Stravinsky undertook his customary European tour, with the difference that for much of the time he was filmed by CBS Television, who were making a documentary about him. We thus have a record of his visit to the Théâtre du Champs-Elysées, where *The Rite* was first performed 52 years earlier, and to Les Tilleuls, the Clarens *pension* where it was composed. The trip also took in Poland, where he conducted in Warsaw and visited Chopin's birthplace, but, to his chagrin, was denied permission by the authorities to travel to Ustilug, which was now in Polish territory. In June, he was the guest of the new Pope Paul VI at a concert in the

T S Eliot (1888–1965), whose death prompted Stravinsky's *Introitus*

Vatican, of which his *Symphony of Psalms* formed the centrepiece, and in September gave concerts in London. Around these engagements, he continued to make and supervise recordings of his works in Hollywood.

'All my contemporaries are dead': Stravinsky at 83

Despite his age and increasing frailty, the round of concert-giving and recordings continued into 1966, taking him to Minneapolis, St Louis, San Francisco, Paris, Athens and Lisbon. He also went to New York for the Stravinsky Festival which was held at the Lincoln Center during June and July, one of the notable events of which was a performance of *The Soldier's Tale* featuring three of his most celebrated younger contemporaries, Elliott Carter (as the Soldier), Aaron Copland (the Narrator) and John Cage (the Devil). He was also approached in a restaurant by Frank Sinatra, who asked him for his autograph.

But the years were beginning to take their toll. Asked by one interviewer how it felt to be 84, he replied:

'I am forgetful, repetitive, and deaf, for which reason I tend to avoid all but Russian language conversations and in consequence to read more than ever before... A still more serious complaint than these, to me, is the diminishing of my working day, for though my composing speed is unslackened, the time allotted to it, due to the slow tempo of my other activities and to the greater demands on my time from lawyers, merchants, and especially doctors, evaporates more quickly...

'I suffer, too, as rarely before and as I have never admitted, from my musical isolation, as well as from a feeling of loneliness – this for the first time in my life – for my generation: all of my contemporaries are dead.'

On 13 August, back in Los Angeles, he finished the *Requiem Canticles*, on which he had been working, as time and health allowed, for the last year and a half. He described it as the first 'pocket-requiem' – it sets only parts of the Latin Mass for the Dead and lasts a mere 15 minutes – and would apparently have called it *Sinfonia da Requiem* had he not 'shared too many titles and subjects with Mr Britten already' (though 'Canticles' is of course no less redolent of Britten). As he foresaw, it has proved the most accessible of the works of his last period, and is indeed one of the most immediate in impact of any of his sacred pieces. Set for contralto and bass soloists, chorus and orchestra, it is introduced by an instrumental 'Prelude' in which the strings make urgent play of repeated notes. After the 'Exaudi' and the appropriately dramatic 'Dies Irae' and 'Tuba Mirum', there is another instrumental movement, an 'Interlude' of great repose for wind and timpani. The ensuing 'Rex Tremendae' seems to allude to the six-note rhythmic motif in the last movement of the *Symphony of Psalms*, and the 'Libera Me' – the only movement in which the Requiem text is set in its entirety – is perhaps the most powerful instance of unpitched chanting in all of Stravinsky's late works, the quartet of soloists singing in the foreground while the choir whisper the words behind them. The work ends with a 'Postlude' for percussion alone which stands as a kind of apotheosis of Stravinsky's time-suspending codas over the years, from the 'Canticle' of the *Three Pieces for String Quartet*, through the chorale of the *Symphonies of Wind Instruments* to the 'Epilogue' of *The Fairy's Kiss*. Above all, in its repeated chimes, leading to the final sustained 'chord of death', it recalls the last miraculous bars of *The Wedding*.

Even as he was composing it, Stravinsky drew an explicit parallel between his *Requiem Canticles* and Mozart's famously valedictory *Requiem*. Though it is formally dedicated to the memory of Helen Buchanan Seeger, at 84 and in ever-declining health, he knew he was writing it also for himself. In the event, though, it was not his physical but his creative life that the *Canticles* would memorialise. There was to be only one more original composition, a setting for soprano and piano of Edward Lear's poem *The Owl and the Pussy-cat*, which Stravinsky described as a 'musical sigh of relief' after the labour of the *Canticles*. The song is dedicated to Vera, its text being the first English poem she ever learnt by heart. And it is with this touching miniature, a token of his love for the woman who had shared his life for the last 45 years, and would share it for the remaining five, that Stravinsky's long career as a composer came to an end.

Chapter 11

The last years (1967-1971)

The final years of Stravinsky's life are a distressing story of sickness and failing powers, an inexorable decline made all the harder to bear by the undiminished acuity of the intellect with which he observed it. They were also a period of family breakdown, as relations between the composer and his children, strained since the beginning of his affair with Vera in the 1920s, finally collapsed amid bitter accusations of neglect and financial irregularity. Above all, they were years dominated by the agonising recognition, long resisted but eventually inescapable, that he would never again be able to compose.

In January 1967, he made his last recording, of the 1945 *Firebird* suite, and in May conducted his last concert, a performance of the suite from *Pulcinella*. He was admitted to hospital in August with a bleeding stomach ulcer, and again in November with a discoloured hand, which proved to be the precursor of a serious thrombosis. Semi-delirious during this latter stay, he was heard to say 'I have left my passport behind and cannot return' – the *cri de coeur* of a lifelong exile.

His attendance at a performance of the *Requiem Canticles* in Oakland in February 1968 was his first public appearance for nine months, but later the same year he was well enough to travel to San Francisco where, in a single afternoon in May, he arranged two of Hugo Wolf's sacred songs for soprano and chamber ensemble, his last completed work.

At the end of 1968 he flew to Zurich and spent a month in Switzerland, where he worked on a new composition and attempted to impose some order on his unravelling financial affairs by visiting his bank in Basel and revising his will to make Vera the sole beneficiary. He then travelled to Paris for a lively couple of weeks, somewhat after the old dispensation, during which he went sightseeing, caught up with old friends and attended a performance of *The Rite of Spring* at the Opera

House – the last concert of his own music he would hear. 1968 was a brief respite, however, from the health problems which would dog him until his death, sapping his strength and eroding his capacity for creative work.

Some of the most heart-breaking passages in the later conversation books are concerned with the effects of old age, and paint a picture of a proud man finally having to face the fact that, while his mind remained that of a person in his prime, his failing body would henceforth determine the shape of his life. Stravinsky's powers of recovery astonished his doctors. 'I have never seen such inner vitality and force', said one of the most trusted of the phalanx of medicos who, together with a succession of nurses, were charged with the difficult task of caring for him during these final years. But the composer's indomitable will was no longer able to keep at bay the 'loss of combustion' he increasingly felt in respect of his work. 'For me, as a creative musician,' he had once written, 'composition is a daily function that I feel compelled to discharge. I compose because I am made for that and cannot do otherwise.' Tortured, like Haydn in his last years, by the knowledge that he had more music to give, and by musical ideas he no longer had the energy or the concentration to develop, he felt the central purpose of his life had been taken away. One night, for example, he dreamed a new episode in a work-in-progress, but realised when he woke that he couldn't walk to his desk to write it down and that it would be lost to his memory by morning. He fought to retain his working régime, defying pain and weakness to orchestrate parts of Bach's *Well-tempered Clavier*, but with each new crisis in his health the prospect of resuming composition receded further. On his eighty-seventh birthday, newly discharged from hospital after two emergency operations on his leg and unable to sleep because he was 'afraid of dreaming music', he seems finally to have admitted to himself that his creative life was over.

By now, the house at North Wetherly Drive was proving impracticable both for Stravinsky and for Vera, on whom, at 81, the strain of looking after her husband was beginning to tell. In October 1969, after almost three decades on the West Coast, the Stravinskys finally left California and, together with Robert Craft, who had effectively put his own career on hold to help care for the composer, moved to New York. Here, they installed themselves in a characterless suite in the Essex House, where one of their first visitors was Svetlana Stalin Alleluyeva, the daughter of the former dictator.

'The great exemplary artist of the twentieth century': conducting in 1965 – a characteristic image of Stravinsky's later years

At the same time, Stravinsky's life was coming to be dominated by a dispute with his children which resulted, by the time of his death, in a complete breakdown in relations between his first and second families. To judge by Stravinsky's published writings, his surviving children appear to have remained on the emotional periphery of his life. As early as 1916, Nijinsky had commented on the almost military

Death had long been a taboo subject in the Stravinsky household, and the composer had left no instructions as to where he should be buried. Vera had already made arrangements, however, for him to be interred in Venice, the city he loved best after his native St Petersburg. On 15 April, his funeral was held in the church of Santi Giovanni e Paolo in the presence of some 3,000 mourners, while hundreds more thronged the Piazza outside. After the Orthodox service, during which Robert Craft conducted the *Requiem Canticles*, the coffin was taken by water-hearse to the island of San Michele where Stravinsky was laid to rest near the tomb of Diaghilev.

The final resting place: the island of San Michele

'When I die,' Stravinsky had once said, 'I leave you my music... It is music that followed rules that were not written, but I hope I have added something new to what was existing.' Among the many voices contending to assess the significance of the composer's legacy in the immediate aftermath of his death, that of W H Auden, his friend and collaborator, is perhaps the most resonant: 'Stravinsky's career as a composer,' he wrote, 'is as good a demonstration as any that I know of the difference between a major and a minor artist... A major artist is always newly finding himself, so that the history of his works recapitulates or mirrors the history of art. Once he has done something to his satisfaction, he attempts to do something he has never done before. It is only when he is dead that we are able to see that his various creations, taken together, form one consistent oeuvre.' For Auden, as for so many, Stravinsky was 'the great exemplary artist of the twentieth century'. It is a view unlikely to be rescinded as we begin for the first time to see that century too as a completed whole.

Further reading

This book has referred a number of times to Stravinsky's autobiography and to the 'conversation books' published in collaboration with Robert Craft towards the end of the composer's life. Together with Craft's diary and the other works he has written or compiled since the composer's death, they provide the fullest first-hand account of Stravinsky's life and work, and are essential reading for anyone interested in making a closer acquaintance with the composer and his world. Some of the conversation books originally included excerpts from Craft's diary; the following listing gives only the revised editions, which omitted these excerpts and combined two of the original titles into one. The five resulting titles are listed below in the order in which they were originally compiled. Craft's diary was subsequently published as *Stravinsky: Chronicle of a Friendship*.

Works by Stravinsky:

An Autobiography (London & New York, 1936)

Poetics of Music (Cambridge, Mass., 1947)

(Both works were originally published in French, as *Chroniques de ma vie* and *Poétique musicale*.)

Works by Stravinsky and Robert Craft:

Conversations with Igor Stravinsky (London & New York, 1959)

Memories and Commentaries (London & New York, 1960)

Expositions and Developments (London & New York, 1962)

Themes and Conclusions (London, 1972)

Dialogues (London, 1982)

(The penultimate book was originally published as two separate titles, *Themes and Episodes* and *Retrospectives and Conclusions*; the last as *Dialogues and a Diary*.)

Works by Vera Stravinsky and Robert Craft:

Stravinsky in Pictures and Documents (London, 1979; New York, 1978)

Works by Robert Craft:

Stravinsky: Chronicle of a Friendship (Nashville & London, 1994)

Stravinsky: Glimpses of a Life (London, 1992)

A Stravinsky Scrapbook, 1940-1971 (London, 1983)

Igor and Vera Stravinsky: A Photograph Album (London, 1982)

Stravinsky: Selected Correspondence (3 vols, London, 1982, 1984, 1985)

Dearest Bubushkin: Selected Letters and Diaries of Vera and Igor Stravinsky (London, 1985)

Biographies:

The most accessible biographies of Stravinsky are:

Griffiths, Paul *Stravinsky* (in the 'Master Musicians' series; London, 1992)

Oliver, Michael *Igor Stravinsky* (in the '20th-century composers' series; London, 1995)

White, Eric Walter & Noble, Jeremy 'Igor Stravinsky' (in *The New Grove Modern Masters*; London, 1984)

The first volume of Stephen Walsh's biography of Stravinsky is expected at the time of going to press

Studies of the music:

There is of course a vast analytical literature devoted to Stravinsky's music, much of it highly technical in nature. The classic studies most accessible to the non-specialist are:

Vlad, Roman *Stravinsky* (3rd ed., Oxford 1978)

Walsh, Stephen *The Music of Stravinsky* (Oxford, 1988)

White, Eric Walter *Stravinsky: The Composer and his Works* (2nd ed., London 1979)

(In addition to these general studies, the last of which contains an extended biographical introduction, there are some accessible studies of individual works, such as Stephen Walsh's *Oedipus Rex* in the 'Cambridge Music Handbooks' series.)

Stravinsky's recordings of Stravinsky

Stravinsky was among the first composers to grasp the potential of the gramophone. He recorded the majority of his own music, and almost all his major works, either as conductor or pianist or, in the final years, as supervisor to the conducting of Robert Craft, and once described his recordings as 'indispensable supplements to the printed music'. Performance and recording standards are variable, but the series as a whole is one of the great achievements of the gramophone age and represents an invaluable legacy by a composer notoriously suspicious of other performers' 'interpretations' of his work. In many cases, Stravinsky's versions remain far the most impressive in the catalogue, quite apart from their unique value as the composer's own realisations.

Most of his work in the recording studio was done with Columbia Records from the 1930s, and especially in the late 1950s and 1960s, and has now been released by Sony in a 12-volume, 22-disc series, *The Stravinsky Edition*. Available both as a boxed set and as individual volumes, the series also includes recordings of Stravinsky in rehearsal and excerpts from the CBS documentary made during the composer's 1965 European tour (see page 185).

In the details which follow, the works in each volume are listed in alphabetical order of the titles used in this book:

Volume 1: Ballets, etc:
The Firebird
Fireworks
Petrushka
Renard
The Rite of Spring
Scherzo à la russe
Scherzo fantastique
The Soldier's Tale
The Wedding
(SM3K 46291)

Volume 2: Ballets, etc:
Agon
Apollo
Bluebird pas de deux

The Fairy's Kiss
Jeu de cartes
Orpheus
Pulcinella
Scènes de ballet
(SM3K 46292)

Volume 3: Ballet suites:
The Firebird
Petrushka
Pulcinella
(SMK 45293)

Volume 4: Symphonies:
Symphony in C
Symphony in E Flat Major
Symphony in Three Movements
Symphony of Psalms
(Plus Stravinsky in rehearsal, etc.)
(SM2K 46294)

Volume 5: Concertos:
Capriccio
Concerto for Piano and Wind Instruments
Movements
Violin Concerto
(SMK 46295)

Volume 6: Miniature masterpieces:
Circus Polka
Concerto in D 'Basle'
Concerto in E Flat 'Dumbarton Oaks'
Eight Instrumental Miniatures
Four Studies for Orchestra
Four Norwegian Moods
Greeting Prelude
Suites 1 and 2 for Small Orchestra
(SMK 46296)

Volume 7: Chamber music and historical recordings:
Concertino for 12 Instruments
Concerto for Two Solo Pianos
Duo Concertant
Ebony Concerto
Octet

Pastorale
Piano-rag-music
Praeludium
Ragtime for 11 Instruments
Serenade in A
Septet
Sonata for Piano
Sonata for Two Pianos
Symphonies of Wind Instruments
Tango
(SM2K 46297)

Volume 8: Operas [and songs]:
Operas:
Mavra
The Nightingale
Songs:
Cat's Cradle Songs
Elegy for J.F.K.
The Faun and the Shepherdess
Four Russian Peasant Songs
Four Songs
In Memoriam Dylan Thomas
The Owl and the Pussy-cat
Pribaoutki
Three Japanese Lyrics
Three Little Songs 'Recollections of Childhood'
Three Songs from William Shakespeare
'Tilim-bom' (from *Three Tales for Children*)
Two Poems by Balmont
Two Poems of Verlaine
(SM2K 46298)

Volume 9:
The Rake's Progress
(SM2K 46299)

Volume 10: Oratorio – Melodrama:
The Flood
Monumentum pro Gesualdo di Venosa
Ode
Oedipus Rex
Persephone
(SM2K 46300)

Volume 11: Sacred works:
Anthem
Ave Maria
Babel
Cantata
Canticum Sacrum
Chorale-Variations on Vom Himmel hoch
Credo
Introitus
Mass
Pater noster
A Sermon, a Narrative and a Prayer
Threni
Zvezdoliki
(SM2K 46301)

Volume 12: Robert Craft conducts:
Abraham and Isaac
Danses concertantes
Double Canon
Epitaphium
Variations Aldous Huxley in Memoriam
Requiem Canticles
Song of the Nightingale
(SM2K 46302)

Index

*Illustrations are indicated in **bold** type*